JAZZ PIANO FROM SCRATCH
A HOW-TO GUIDE FOR STUDENTS AND TEACHERS

Charles Beale

The Associated Board of the Royal Schools of Music

First published in 1998 by The Associated Board of the Royal Schools of Music (Publishing) Ltd
Reprinted 1998, 2000, 2002, 2005, 2009

Not for sale in the U.S.A.

© 1998 by The Associated Board of the Royal Schools of Music

ISBN 1 86096 015 4

Music and text origination by Barnes Music Engraving, East Sussex.
Printed by Caligraving Ltd, Thetford, Norfolk.

Preface

In assembling the materials for this book, I hope we have been able to reflect some kind of emerging consensus, as well as start a debate. Putting it together has been a long and complex team effort and, like all worthwhile projects, it has been a learning experience for everyone concerned. Three years ago, we wouldn't have been able to define what we meant by Grade 1 jazz improvisation; now we think we can.

Rather than try to say anything startlingly new, we have aimed to synthesize the best practice from classrooms, workshops and jam sessions from around the country. We are setting new standards and also establishing a fresh approach nationally to the teaching and learning of jazz. It is most unlikely that everyone will agree with every word, and indeed, I would be rather disappointed if they did. But I hope that consultation has been wide enough for at least the majority of jazz musicians and educators to recognize something in the ideas and find them useful and practical in their work. I hope, too, that teachers and learners will find this book accessible and clear. Above all, I hope they will be challenged to be creative in using it.

Heartfelt thanks are due to Michael Garrick, Eddie Harvey and Richard Michael, for their long experience, their honesty, their unfailing support, and for contributing at various points substantial chunks of the raw material of the book. Thanks are also due to the many people who read and commented on drafts, in particular Trevor Tomkins, Pete Churchill, Nikki Iles, Barak Schmool, Mike Welsh and Kevin Jackson, all of whom steered the book in important ways. Special thanks to Trevor Tomkins for allowing the Board to use several of his rhythm charts. To the staff and students at Brunel, my thanks for giving me the time to write, and for acting as willing guinea-pigs to my ideas. My thanks also to Philip Mundey, David Blackwell and Kathryn Oswald at the Associated Board. And finally, my thanks to Yuwrajh, for putting up with all my nonsense.

British jazz education is full of pioneers, committed and determined musicians who believe in what they do, and they have rarely been given their due in the past for the important contribution they make to the many lives they touch. As someone whose life has been touched in the past by their love for jazz, I hope all those who read this book will feel that at least something of the free spirit of the music we all love and believe in has been captured but not caged in its pages.

Charles Beale
June 1997

Contents

Introduction

Jazz is not just 'Well, man, this is what I feel like playing'. It's a very structured thing that comes down from a tradition and requires a lot of thought and study.

WYNTON MARSALIS

Welcome to *Jazz Piano from Scratch*. This book is intended for anyone interested in learning jazz piano from the very beginning. Perhaps you are a potential student, with little knowledge but some enthusiasm, or perhaps you already play classical music and want to learn how to play jazz too. You may be a teacher, wanting to learn new skills over the shoulder of your pupils, so you can prepare them better for our new jazz exams. Or perhaps you are just generally interested and musical but have never had the courage to attempt jazz before. Whatever you are, this book is a simple, practical, step-by-step introduction to the discipline and free spirit of jazz playing. If you're willing to put in the work, it should be an enjoyable read, and will give you the skills and understanding you need to get started.

As a jazz teacher, workshop leader and attender of summer schools, I find the question everyone asks is what book to buy. Other jazz books can often seem complex and full of jargon, intended perhaps for more advanced players or those who already have a basic grasp of the style. We hope this one plugs a gap because it starts from the very beginning. Through a structured series of activities, it will lead you into jazz playing and improvising, building early confidence through getting an initial flow of musical ideas going, and then gradually adding in the various elements that will give your jazz playing a solid rhythmic, melodic and harmonic foundation. It is the product of a long consultation process, and top jazz educators nationally have contributed their ideas and experience—we feel confident this tried and tested approach will work for you!

There are some other important first principles. This book is not something you can read in an armchair—you need to be by a piano and preferably with a friend or teacher, ready to sing, clap or play. It's full of musical things to do, because in jazz you show you understand how to play by playing.

Secondly, the best way to learn to play jazz is by listening to other players and imitating them. So if you have a CD player, put it by the piano if you can. We've provided references to various CDs and recordings, names of key players and styles, for you to follow up. We've also provided our own CD with this book, where professional players and teachers give examples of the sound-world, go through a number of the exercises and demonstrate the key styles in simple ways. Listen to it carefully because it is the *sound* of the music that's most important—the CD is as important as the book itself. The relevant track is indicated in the CD symbol alongside the example or activity.

Finally this book, like the graded books of pieces, is designed for anyone wanting to learn jazz piano and not simply those wishing to enter the Associated Board jazz piano exams. Of course, if you want to enter for the exams, this book will help you, and indeed the short final section (Part III) goes through the exam in detail, giving pointers and showing you how to prepare and what examiners will be looking for. But the bulk of the book is actually simply about playing jazz piano itself, about what the skills are and how to acquire them in an enjoyable and progressive way. The pieces in the graded books cover all the main styles, from the early masters to the present day. They have been designed to be played outside the exam context as well as within it, so you can play them in school concerts or even at your own gigs. Many of the music examples in this book are taken from these pieces and you may find it helpful to work through the books of pieces and this book at the same time.

The book is in three parts. Part I, 'Starting Out', leads the absolute beginner progressively through simple but effective musical games and exercises to introduce the main concepts, and takes the learner from scratch through to approximately Grade 3. This is followed by more advanced chapters in Part II, 'Moving On', which build on initial progress and suggest ways of exploring the musical materials of jazz in more depth. Part III, 'Preparing for the Exam', focuses specifically on the exam itself and on the needs of candidates and the teachers who prepare them.

At the head of each chapter and part you'll find a quotation about jazz. These represent a range of opinion: some are quotations from jazz musicians or composers; some give a view from the past. Some give useful advice, some will make you think, and some—we hope!—will make you laugh.

Before we get into the detail, here are some tips to help you to make quicker progress:

1   Practise your instrument regularly. Do at least some practice every day to gain the flexibility you need to become really expressive. In particular sing what you play, play what you sing, and listen carefully to what you play, making continual improvements. Try recording yourself from time to time so you can really listen hard to how you sound. Each practice session should include some warm-up rhythm exercises, some scales, some doodling, some work by ear and from notation and definitely some improvising!

2   Listen closely to recordings, and sing or play them back. Close study of a recording, and direct imitation on an instrument or by singing the line, is the only way to work out how many jazz effects are done; even if it's only by repeating your favourite two bars over and over again to begin with. Indulge your own musical obsessions, and get deeply into the playing of key musicians (use our Listening Guide as a start)—hum their tunes in the shower, play their recordings in your bedroom, in the car or on your walkman, immerse yourself in the sounds.

3   Get into a band with some friends. There is no better motivation to practise than to be playing regularly with others, once a week or more—it brings the music alive by re-creating the classics, or making up your own tunes. Jazz is a music which often occurs in groups, and you will learn at least as much from

playing with others as you will from books or notated music.

4   Find a teacher or mentor. A 'critical friend', someone who really understands the style, can save you a lot of trial and error by inspiring you and pointing you in the right direction. If you are really dedicated, it may only take a few lessons, or one now and then, but all jazz musicians will tell you that the odd piece of advice from a respected fellow musician is invaluable. Attendance at workshops, summer schools and other short courses can also be a great help.

5   Go to hear jazz musicians play. Whenever possible, get out there and hear the real thing live. Enjoy the vibrancy and emotion of the sounds, feel the communication, follow a player who you really like, share your enthusiasm with others.

6   Work regularly on your musical memory. As you learn, you will be continually involved in identifying, absorbing, reproducing and generally internalizing rhythms, melodies and chord sequences, singing them to get them in your ear, and using them in structured improvisation. Musical learning in jazz depends crucially on having a good musical memory.

Finding your own way

Many prominent jazz musicians taught themselves mainly by playing in bands in constant interaction with others, listening and imitating them. This is undoubtedly the best way.

Learning to play jazz is in that sense rather like learning a language. When learning to talk, we are not taught too many organizing principles to begin with. Instead we learn to speak through trial and error, by listening hard to what others say and by asking questions when we are ready to learn something or where we don't understand. If someone stopped us every time we made a mistake in the early stages, perhaps we would never learn to speak at all!

The same process should be at work as you learn to play jazz. This book is designed to get the musical flow going confidently—the learning should then happen naturally. The grammar of the harmony and the rhythm of jazz will emerge gradually in your development and can then be tightened up and formalized through your own recognition of the structures that underlie what you do.

Being 'on the edge'

In any kind of improvising, we have no choice but to learn by making mistakes. Making mistakes fosters the self-awareness from which we begin to discover what we need to learn next, or to paraphrase a famous quotation from Miles Davis, every jazz performance, however polished, is in that sense a rehearsal, a chance to try something new, to take a risk. Of course jazz musicians set themselves high standards, but they do this by finding their own musical boundaries and then striving to break through them, to play even more inventively or with even more technical assurance than before.

So we end with an entreaty to push yourself as a musician, to find your own limitations and then conquer them, to make hundreds of confident mistakes, and so to learn from them. The more you become aware of your own areas of strength and weakness, the easier it is to practise effectively, to solve the problems and to make swift progress. This is both an enjoyable and a frightening process, and makes for music and learning that is always exciting, dynamic and 'on the edge'.

But then again, you can do what the hell you like . . .

EDDIE HARVEY

Part I
STARTING OUT

Feel the fear and do it anyway

SUSAN JEFFERS

Chapter 1

Opening Rhythm Workshops

Has anyone ever heard a metronome that made you want to dance?

TREVOR TOMKINS (drummer)

Jazz begins and ends as rhythm. Understand the rhythmic language of jazz and the rest will take care of itself. So we begin with a set of simple rhythm games and exercises, which are fun to do, feel natural and will get you moving, both literally and metaphorically.

Use these workshop exercises as the basis of five minutes regular rhythm work in every practice session. Once you have the basics under your belt, you'll find ways of developing them further for yourself, to practise rhythmic improvising on particular pieces. They will help you understand why the rhythms in the given parts sound as they do, and help you play the given music stylishly and in time. Come back and dip into this chapter regularly once you get going on the rest of the book, and remember, you are not expected to finish this chapter before moving on to the rest of Part I.

Workshop 1: Feel the beat

From the very start always be physically and mentally positive and energetic in your rhythm. Don't hold back! Consciously put aside any inhibitions, and move your body gently but positively and dance along with the pulses and rhythms you make. Try to get the rhythms into your body as well as your head, literally to *feel* the rhythm through the movement of your limbs; your learning will then become more effective as well as more enjoyable. Learning to let yourself go bodily is as much part of the process in jazz as developing musical self-discipline, and the ideal jazz musician achieves both: a controlled but relaxed ease with the music.

Activities

1 Listen carefully to the piece of music given on track 1 on the CD. As you listen, clap along or tap on the table or dance around.
Don't worry too much about being in strict time to begin with—just feel the beat and move your body along with it.

2 Now listen again and focus on the beat itself. Clap, tap and move along with it evenly and positively, but always in a relaxed fashion.

3 Once you have the pulse clear in your mind, tap on every beat (crotchets), then every two beats (minims), and finally twice within every beat (quavers).

4   Now turn the CD off and tap the same pulse again on your own, for about a minute. Consciously use your own sense of pulse or internal clock, rather than relying on the music for a lead. Turn the CD back on. Did you keep the same speed?

5   Work at keeping a steady pulse going with other recordings at a range of speeds, and perhaps alter the way you move to fit the character of the music. It should be easier when you make the pulse more explicit, perhaps swaying with bigger movements or stamping with positive confidence. Did you rush or drag? Were you relaxed?

One way to tell how relaxed you were is to listen to your breathing. You may find you hold your breath or take quick and shallow breaths at certain points—both signs of tension. Try to ensure you breathe out as well as in as you play, and take breaths as you would naturally. Sometimes breathing deeply can help as part of a warm-up routine.

Also look for signs of tension in your body, which may interfere later with your playing. How are your shoulders and your neck? Were you tapping your foot with great intensity and tensing all your leg muscles? Again, the more you can use your body in an efficient and relaxed way, the more responsive and undistracted your mind and body will be once you begin to improvise.

6   As you hear recordings and performances of a range of music in jazz, rock or latin styles, begin consciously to tap, sing and move along with them—feel the beat. Try and get a sense of the particular rhythmic character of the music you hear, and relate that to how you might dance to it. The way you respond personally will relate directly to how you improvise later. Choose music in a variety of styles, moods, tempos and feels (we'll come to what this means in a few pages), including some that you know and enjoy and others recommended to you. You'll also find doing the rhythm exercises in this chapter along with some real music is more satisfying.

7   Now listen carefully to track 2 and pick out a simple repeated rhythm. Tap and clap along with it, until you can do so accurately. Listen to other jazz recordings and pick out a simple rhythm you can hear on a particular instrument—perhaps the bass-line or a percussion instrument.

8   Listen again. Were all the notes in your rhythm at the same dynamic or were some stressed more than others? Were some longer or shorter than others? Were some damped while others were allowed to ring? Try and imitate the phrasing, dynamics and character of the rhythms you hear as well as their placement from the very beginning.

9   Finally, try making up your own regular one- or two-bar rhythm that fits with the groove you hear, and clap along with it. Perhaps find a rhythm similar to one you like from what you hear, or invent a totally new one of your own.

Often the rhythmic character or **groove** of a piece of music is defined by the bass-line. Is it smooth and pulsing, like a crotchet walking bass (track 3), or a complex, funky one, with offbeats, accents and spaces in unexpected places and a variety of long and short notes (track 4)? Does it repeat? If so, over how many bars?

Workshop 2: Group pulse

When musicians play together in a group, they must all be going along at the same speed and must feel the beat together. In jazz this means they have to synchronize their own **internal clock** with the other musicians. The raw emotive power of a whole group pulsing as one is often the feature that strikes many listeners first about jazz and other popular musics, before they become aware of any musical detail.

This can be achieved through careful technique, co-ordination and above all by listening to other players. Accomplished jazz musicians can feel a pulse, play with and against it, and invent ideas which interact and interlock with other rhythms. They listen hard and count, initially out loud and later in their heads, until it becomes instinctive. Without a solid internal clock the whole process is impossible—a jazz musician without good time and good listening skills is not a good jazz musician.

The same need for a good internal clock applies to playing solo piano. The rhythmic freedom of right-hand melody can only be felt against a really solid inner sense of where the beat is in a left-hand rhythm part.

Activities

1 In a pair, a group, or alone with a metronome, start a steady pulse, perhaps at about crotchet = 120, but later at slower and faster tempos too. If in a group of two, clap, tap or stamp on alternate beats like this, and count your beat out loud along with your clapping:

First person says and claps: 1 3

Second person says and claps: 2 4
   (or metronome)

Now swap around, taking the other's part. If in three or more, decide your own way of working—perhaps each repeating the same beat. Then try the same in patterns of three and eventually even five beats.

Listen carefully to yourself and others as you work. Were you early or late? Could you support another person, by helping them place their beat? Do *you* have problems at any point? Ask others what they hear. Use your eyes as well as your ears to synchronize with them exactly—watch their hands or, if a leader is using instruments, watch the movement of the sticks against the cymbal or drum. Tap along with them on the troublesome beat. Aim for complete synchronization, moving as one person.

2 Practise until you can get a steady group pulse going at a range of different speeds in both three and four time, and again clapping along with recordings of favourite performers. Get used to the feeling of *co-ordination* this exercise involves. You must listen to the other person in order to be in time with them, and they must also listen equally hard to you.

3 Make up variations on this theme for yourself. Perhaps invent more complex rhythms out of two simple ones, or use a metronome as the basis of a groove, and then invent a pattern that interlocks with it interestingly. Try using a range of body sounds or the voice. If in a pair, perhaps be a drum-kit between the two of you, making several interlocking rhythms—one person be the bass-drum while another is the hi-hat; if there are three of you, let the third be the snare. If so inclined, make up a set of movements to go with your rhythms. If you have a drum machine or a sequencer, put in one pattern and invent another to play live against it.

Workshop 3: Subdividing the pulse

Did you notice that when you worked at slower tempos, and the spaces between the beats got larger, you found it harder to stay in time? To solve this problem, musicians of all styles *subdivide* the pulse as they count. This involves dividing each beat up into either two or three smaller segments. Begin to count these segments as well as the main beats, and you will find keeping in time and placing on- and offbeat rhythms at all speeds is easier.

In jazz there are many kinds of subdivision of great subtlety. No two players will feel the beat in exactly the same way, and it is this that gives each performance its individual character. Broadly, however, we can think of two kinds of subdivision, also known as **feel**.

Sometimes players divide each beat up into *two* (even quavers):

This feel is known as **straight 8s**, or sometimes as straight or even quavers.

And sometimes they subdivide the beat into *three* (triplets):

We suggest you call this feel simply **swing**, though you may sometimes find it called 'jazz quavers' (or, in classical music, compound time). As with many of these jazz conventions, the real world contains more than one set of names.*

On track 6 the players switch from straight 8s to a swing feel to show the difference between the two. At its very simplest, triplet subdivisions are the basis of all swing feels used in jazz, while even quavers or straight 8s are the basis of many rock and latin grooves.

---

* The word swing can also imply a particular style of jazz first made popular in the 1930s. Used as a feel indication, however, swing can be applied to music from any period and with any other stylistic characteristics, simply implying a basic triplet feel.

Activities

Here are some practice routines to do in these feels. Start at about crotchet = 90. Once you have them under your belt, invent your own variations.

1   In the first, say the subdivisions in straight 8s and clap different parts of the bar as shown.

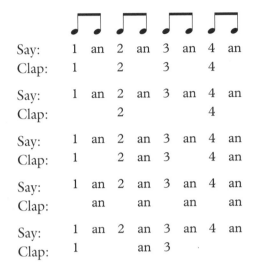

Say:	1	an	2	an	3	an	4	an
Clap:	1		2		3		4	

Say:	1	an	2	an	3	an	4	an
Clap:			2				4	

Say:	1	an	2	an	3	an	4	an
Clap:	1		2	an	3		4	an

Say:	1	an	2	an	3	an	4	an
Clap:		an		an		an		an

Say:	1	an	2	an	3	an	4	an
Clap:	1			an	3			

2   Now repeat at the same tempo, but this time in swing:

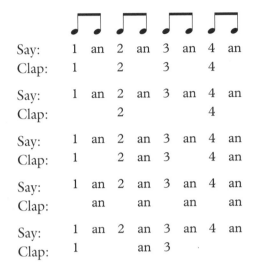

Say:	1	trip - let	2	trip - let	3	trip - let	4	trip - let
Clap:	1		2		3		4	

Say:	1	trip - let	2	trip - let	3	trip - let	4	trip - let
Clap:			2				4	

Say:	1	trip - let	2	trip - let	3	trip - let	4	trip - let
Clap:	1	-let	2	-let	3	-let	4	-let

Say:	1	trip - let	2	trip - let	3	trip - let	4	trip - let
Clap:		-let		-let		-let		-let

Say:	1	trip - let	2	trip - let	3	trip - let	4	trip - let
Clap:	1		2	-let	3		4	-let

This last rhythm is sometimes known as the ten-to-ten rhythm, because that is how it sounds, played on the ride cymbal of a drum-kit. If you hear this rhythm or a variation of it, you know you're dealing with a swing feel.

3   Repeat all these exercises regularly in the early stages at different tempos: *slow* (crotchet = 60–80), *medium* (crotchet = 80–140) and *fast*, usually known as 'up' tempo (crotchet = at least 140).

Notice how working with your voice as well as clapping helps the rhythm. Many people around the world, from North Indian tabla players to Ghanaian drummers, learn rhythms by vocalizing them. Vocalizing rhythms as well as tapping them seems to gel them in the mind, just as singing melodies as well as playing them helps you to learn to pitch—your voice is your instrument and the most direct means of learning to make sounds.

The syllables suggested are conventional to jazz educators and worth learning in themselves. They have been chosen because they are easy to say ('an' not 'and'), because they differentiate rhythms of different types ('one trip-let' versus 'one-an, two-an') and because they work well if repeated round and round. Once you get good at saying the syllables, using pitched voice (singing) is also less of a problem.

To get swing feel into your head, some people find it helps to sing the subdivisions using two pitches, something like this:

da - da - do da - da - do da - da - do da - da - do

The backbeat

In both jazz and rock music there is often a stress on beats 2 and 4, and this stress or emphasis is known as the **backbeat**. It creates an up and down motion within four beats, which you can feel in your body or when you click your fingers, like this:

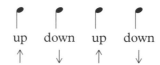

up   down   up   down
↑   ↓   ↑   ↓

Activities

1 Try the above exercises again, this time slightly emphasizing 2 and 4, for example:

in swing:

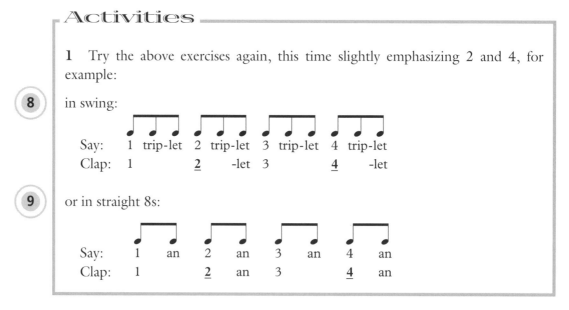

Say:	1	trip-let	2	trip-let	3	trip-let	4	trip-let
Clap:	1		**2**	-let	3		**4**	-let

or in straight 8s:

Say:	1	an	2	an	3	an	4	an
Clap:	1		**2**	an	3		**4**	an

A note about rhythmic notation

Rock and latin grooves are usually notated in simple time and may be played almost as they look, with the quavers played and written in straight 8s. Swing, however, always *sounds* in triplet feel ('one trip-let two trip-let' etc.), but is usually *written* in simple time, as straight 8s in 4/4. The quaver on the third triplet is written as a straight quaver, but sounds on the third of each group of three (on the 'let' in the above examples).

Thus the swing ten-to-ten rhythm as clapped below:

Say: 1 trip-let   2 trip-let   3 trip-let   4 trip-let
Clap: 1   2 -let   3   4 -let

which, in compound time, would be written as:

is notated in jazz like this:

It is left to the jazz player to play this in style with a swing feel.

Partly because it was intended originally to be used in a different style of music, stave notation often fails to capture the expressive elements of the groove, giving only an approximation of the rhythmic outline. For example, even straight feels sometimes have a small degree of triplet feel. Jazz is an aural tradition in that sense, and most of the inflections in the rhythm and melody cannot be easily notated or described in words.

The best way to learn the rhythmic inflection is therefore to spend time regularly listening to the major exponents of each style on recordings or in person, and to imitate directly from recordings—the listening guide at the back of the book will help you here. Listen to the great drummers and improvisers listed, and you'll hear a wide range of timings, inflections and phrasings, all of which come under the broad headings of either swing or straight 8s.

Workshop 4: Swing, rock and latin grooves

The pulse alone has no expressive character—it's simply a way of dividing a bar up at a particular speed. In jazz the music is given character by the repeated rhythms and patterns that the musicians play over the pulse.

This character is achieved in two main ways. Firstly, these rhythms create repeating *stressed* and *unstressed* parts of the bar; for example, there might be a backbeat on beats 2 and 4. Secondly, the repeating rhythms divide each beat into its *subdivisions*, with varying degrees of swing or straight 8s. In jazz and other popular styles every tune has its own individual rhythmic character depending on where the stresses are, how the pulse is subdivided and how the musicians create interesting rhythmic variations around the groove.

Jazz musicians use the word **groove** to refer to a particular rhythmic style or genre. To begin with you need only to be able to distinguish three main types of groove: swing, rock and latin. Even though the jazz piano syllabus does not strictly deal with rock music or latin music as a genre, jazz musicians nowadays often play using rock or latin grooves as well as swing. (Remember from earlier that the word feel is only used when we want to talk generally about subdivisions of the pulse.)

Activities

On the CD are some examples of basic swing, rock, and latin grooves, played by a full rhythm section. Clap along, and feel the difference in character in each case. Listen to how the groove becomes more flexible as the players go into the solo.

10

1 'Bags' Groove' (Milt Jackson). Swing groove, swing feel:

11

2 'I wish I knew how it would feel to be free' (Billy Taylor). Rock groove, straight 8s feel:

12

3 'The Girl from Ipanema' (Antonio Carlos Jobim). Latin groove (actually a bossa nova), straight 8s feel:

We'll look in more detail at the differences between these grooves in Part II.

At the top of each piece printed in the Board's albums of jazz piano pieces you'll find these terms used to indicate the rhythmic style and the type of groove intended. At different tempos, dynamics and levels of intensity, of course, these grooves may be characterized in many different ways. Remember too that jazz is a tradition that has been going for a hundred years, and at various points in its history it has interacted with other popular styles from around the world, including rock music, music from South America and the West Indies, and music from Africa, India and Europe. Each area of the world has its own rhythmic dialect, its own way of subdividing and making stresses, and jazz musicians have absorbed parts of these traditions, and invented their own terms for the rhythms they play.

Workshop 5: Rhythmic placement

Improvising is about making musical choices. In jazz it is rhythmic choices that matter most, and these placement exercises are designed to give you the largest possible number of available rhythmic options, so that you can make your playing sound more distinctive.

Developing rhythmic flexibility is a vital weapon in the jazz musician's armoury. It enables you to choose where to place the start of your phrase, where in the bar to end it, and placement skill also gives you a series of rhythmic possibilities to choose from as you improvise, by, for example, repeating your phrase at a different place in the bar, altering rhythms note by note within a phrase, and so on.

Let's look at some exercises to get you going. Of course, the exercises and techniques introduced here, and which we develop in Part II, take much time and practice to master fully, and seasoned players continue to work regularly on these aspects of their playing to expand further the limits of what they are able to do. But the principles are remarkably simple, and you can get going straight away.

Placing single notes on each beat

Activities

1 Let's begin by simply clapping on each beat of a 4/4 bar in turn while saying the other beats, like this:

Clap	2	3	4	Clap	2	3	4
1	Clap	3	4	1	Clap	3	4
1	2	Clap	4	1	2	Clap	4
1	2	3	Clap	1	2	3	Clap

2 Now try this with the CD. Clap first the beats through the bar and then do the same with some music in a straight 8s feel.

3 Try again, this time speaking the beat to be stressed instead of clapping on it, while saying the other beats quietly or even under your breath:

1	2	3	4	**1**	2	3	4
1	**2**	3	4	1	**2**	3	4
1	2	**3**	4	1	2	**3**	4
1	2	3	**4**	1	2	3	**4**

(With these and all the following exercises, speak as well as clap, so that later you can sing as well as play. Make sure your clapping is even, positive and energetic, but not too loud.)

Placing single notes on the quaver

The next stage is to clap on every *quaver* or upbeat of a 4/4 bar, in both swing and straight feels.

Activities

1 Begin by feeling the subdivisions and saying to yourself round and round:

  1 an 2 an 3 an 4 an | 1 an 2 an 3 an 4 an

or in swing (think the 'trip' but don't say it):

  1 (trip)-let 2 (trip)-let 3 (trip)-let 4 (trip)-let |

  1 (trip)-let 2 (trip)-let 3 (trip)-let 4 (trip)-let

The 'an' or 'let' in each case is the upbeat.

2 Go through each of the subdivisions of the 4/4 bar (and later these in a 3/4 bar too) clapping or speaking on *each quaver* in turn: Try first in straight 8s:

  <u>1</u> an 2 an 3 an 4 an | <u>1</u> an 2 an 3 an 4 an

  1 <u>**an**</u> 2 an 3 an 4 an | 1 <u>**an**</u> 2 an 3 an 4 an

And so on, through all the beats and the 'an ' that follows it. Try speaking all the subdivisions under your breath and only saying loudly the relevant one, if this helps.

3 Now try it in swing, like this:

  <u>1</u> let 2 let 3 let 4 let | <u>1</u> let 2 let 3 let 4 let

  1 <u>**let**</u> 2 let 3 let 4 let | 1 <u>**let**</u> 2 let 3 let 4 let

and so on.

4 Try this exercise in swing with track 14, first clapping the subdivisions through the bar and then doing the same with some music.

It's important to work these sorts of activities in both swing and straight 8s, as we've done here. In the same way, practise all of the following exercises in both feels.

Placing accurately on an upbeat

Some people find it hard to place sounds accurately on the upbeat to begin with. This is often because they fail to relate an upbeat quaver to the downbeat before it. Thus if you wanted to place a sound on the 'an' or the 'let' of one, try practising this by placing a sound on the first beat of the bar too, like this:

Once you can play both the 'one' and the 'an' of 'one' together, try first playing the 'one' more quietly:

---

then saying or stamping the 'one' while clapping or playing the 'an' that follows it:

and finally simply thinking the 'one', but not actually realizing it at all:

All upbeats are in this sense launched from the downbeat that precedes them.

Placement using common rhythms

Once you've mastered placing a single note on any crotchet or quaver of the bar, you can begin to work with little rhythmic phrases, displacing them crotchet by crotchet or quaver by quaver through the bar. Let's begin with two quavers.

Activities

1 Just as with the clapping exercise, try placing this two-note phrase on each beat of the bar, like this:

On beat 1: ♪♪ 2   3   4 | ♪♪ 2   3   4

On beat 2: 1   ♪♪ 3   4 | 1   ♪♪ 3   4

and so on.

2 Once you've mastered this, try the same again, this time transposing through the quavers like this:

1 an 2   3   4 | **1 an 2**   3   4

1 an 2   3   4 | **1 an 2**   3   4

and so on. Say and clap all of these alternatives, in swing and straight feels, and play them on single notes on the keyboard. Listen to track 15 and try this with others clapping and playing.

3 When this is comfortable, try the same thing with some of the following, slightly longer rhythms:

4 Now invent some new ones of your own, initially choosing rhythms with only two or three notes. Play around with them, deciding where in the bar they sound good and where they seem to work less well. Start off with 4/4 alone, but remember to work in 3/4 once you get more confident.

Working with a click

A metronome or drum machine may be useful as a guide or partner in these exercises when you are working alone. The following tips may help:

1 Avoid using a click all the time. There are many young musicians who can play very well if using a click, while their own internal clock runs less reliably!

2 Try setting the metronome or drum machine to click on different beats of the bar, to simulate a variety of grooves. This will force you to fill in elements of the pulse missed out. For example, click on beats 2 and 4, using the metronome for the backbeat only, or click only on beat 1.

3 If working in a group, amplify the sound through an amplifier and speakers to work on the common problem of a whole rhythm section speeding up or slowing down while playing.

4 If you are working with a drum machine, make your preset patterns as musical as possible—find one that allows you to use stressed and unstressed beats, and always leave space for *you* to do the counting! Avoid too dense a texture, as cluttering the whole texture with sounds will prevent you from hearing both yourself and the pulse clearly.

Workshop 6: Question and answer

From the earliest spirituals, 'call and response' or 'question and answer' phrasing has been at the heart of African American musics, as well as being part of Western classical music. Taken up by jazz, it is one of the many parts of the style shared with other musics.

The basic principle is simple: a musical question sets up something unfinished, a stimulus or tension of some kind:

and the musical answer which follows it completes the phrase, balancing the first half with a second half that relates to it in some way:

For some improvisers, question and answer gives structure to what they create. It is also a useful way of learning to improvise for a particular length of time—your question has to last, say, for two bars, and the reply has also to last for two. The framework of a set length of time teaches you to take decisions about when to begin and end your phrases and also to engage in essential listening to another player and to some given material while trying to improvise yourself. In the exams this core skill is assessed specifically in the quick studies and aural tests and developed and extended through the grades.

The first stage is to begin to internalize the pulse and tap along *in our heads*, perhaps just nodding slightly in time with what we hear, as many jazz musicians do, or clicking a finger along with a groove.

1 *Feel a one-bar space and count in your head.* Tap a steady pulse of four in a bar at about 112 beats per minute. Then leave a gap on beats 2, 3 and 4, perhaps initially saying 'two, three, four', then whispering it, and finally leaving out any sounds on the other beats altogether. Don't tap your feet in the gaps, as this may become a handicap to developing physical rhythmic co-ordination later. Try and count it entirely in your head.

Clap   2   3   4 | Clap   2   3   4

Make sure the gap is accurate, and you come back in on the 'one' positively.

2 *Feel a two-bar space and count in your head.* Now leave out the 'one' on every other bar, leaving a gap of seven beats. Think the gap like this:

Clap   2   3   4 | 1   2   3   4

Practise first lightly tapping or saying the other beats, then with complete silence, relying only on your internal clock. This will help you build an awareness of a two-bar gap. Also, try doing this with a friend or in a group. Did you count at the same speed? Did you clap together after the gap?

3 *Clap the question and leave a gap for the answer.* Before you can improvise, you have to be able to leave a gap the right size to improvise in; you have to feel the space. So the next stage is to clap a rhythm, lasting two bars of 4 beats, and then leave a gap, also of two bars, like this:

Swing ♩ = 112

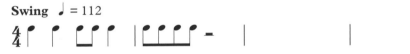

Do this several times, keeping a steady pulse going and coming in confidently after a gap of the right length.

4 *Echo the question.* Now we start to *fill* the gap, firstly by echoing the question. Begin with a two-bar rhythm, perhaps like this one:

Clap it to a partner and then have them clap it back in the next bar. Repeat this several times and keep in strict time throughout, aiming to keep the time going even if you make a mistake. Be sure to copy the given phrase exactly, in feel, phrasing and dynamics, and if you are making up new questions, give them some life by being positive.

This can easily develop into a rhythm game where one person claps a rhythm and the others have to answer it immediately in the following space. You can play this in a pair, round in a circle, sometimes to a click, and perhaps sometimes with real music in the background.

If you are working on your own, the CD provides three examples of grooves at different speeds for you to use as the background to your practice. In each case, we've recorded a few clapped questions to get you started, then keep the groove going for you to clap your own. The grooves are swing (track 18), medium tempo rock (track 19) and fast latin (track 20). If you find your answering rhythms hard in the faster examples, clap very simply.

Use a tape recorder to record your own new sets of questions to a click if you need to, and then play the tape back, echoing and later answering in the gaps you have left.

5 *Clap and fill the gap with your own answer.* Once you can count the gap accurately and copy a given phrase, you can begin to make up your own answer to the question asked, like this:

Try these other two-bar questions, clapping them and providing answers in the gaps.

After a few sessions, and once you can feel the length of a two-bar phrase and improvise in a number of different ways within it, work up to improvisations of four bars. But don't make the exercise longer until your improvisations at the previous length are in complete, discrete phrases which begin and end musically, and when you feel you can be flexible with them. Accept *no* unfocused improvising from yourself or others—if you feel you're floundering, reduce the amount of available space again to a manageable size, until you know you can count it accurately *and* improvise within the space with ease.

Question and answer also helps you count through a long form. Later on we'll introduce the twelve-bar blues, which is of course twelve bars long! At this stage it is worth practising two-bar questions and answers in groups of three as follows:

1		2		3	
question	answer	question	answer	question	answer
2 bars	2 bars	2 bars	2 bars	2 bars	2 bars

This will help you count and so feel the length of a chorus in twelve bars, and is good preparation for improvising the blues.

Use this technique also when preparing the improvisation sections of the pieces, where in the solo section you should look carefully to see how long each chorus is, and what the possibilities are for dividing it up. Typical forms will be eight and sixteen bars long. Of course you can divide up your solo in many different ways and variety is to be encouraged, but a good starting-point might be to divide it into lengths of two and four bars, and treat other approaches as variations on this.

Workshop 7: Extending these activities

All of the above exercises stress rhythm, but it is also vital to improvise with musical character even in the early stages. In order to keep your practice varied and above all expressive, try all of the above exercises with some of the variations below, which bring in other musical elements. Many are suitable to be done in groups as well as alone, and the enjoyment and learning gained by working in interaction with others is immense, particularly because working with others you have to listen. Try, for example, to contrast with what the previous person did, or to complement it.

Above all, aim to produce a sound which is *distinctive* and which will stand out from the crowd. Strive always for an improvisation that has individuality.

Activities

1 *Exploring dynamics, texture and levels of intensity.* Try alternating loud with soft improvisations. Use accents and subtractions from the stresses to create variety of shading in your phrases. Use extremes of very loud and very soft, very fast or very slow phrases, very full or very empty, to establish the very limits of what your instrument or clapping will produce. In jazz you can often increase the dynamic by becoming more intense, playing more densely or leaving more spaces so the notes you do play have power and drama. Be surprising, and explore in turn the outer limits of each parameter: loud, soft, high, low, dense, sparse.

2 *Use of space.* Even with a short rhythm, it's possible to create interesting musical gestures, leaving a long gap at the start, or clapping only once or twice in significant places in the course of a two- or four-bar space. Imitate the understated Miles Davis in a two-bar rhythm improvisation and then try the more verbose style of Dizzy Gillespie, where sometimes every quaver is filled. Again the unexpected will create rhythmic tension, something more interesting to listen to that will grab the ear.

3 *Vary the musical sounds.* Experiment with other body sounds, including stamping, tapping on thighs, then with vocal sounds and (if available) percussion instruments and the piano. Work with combinations of sounds, drum-kit style, with perhaps stamping the foot as the bass-drum, slapping the thighs as the snare and clapping as the hi-hat. Be outrageous in your choice of sounds.

4 *Work slowly from clapping to the piano.* There is more in the following melody

section about applying these rhythm techniques on the piano. But clearly, once the possibilities of basic clapping and so on have been exhausted, begin to apply these exercises to the piano.

5 *Vary the tempo, time signature and feel.* Include fast (up), medium and slow tempos, simple (3/4, 4/4) and compound (6/8, 9/8, 12/8) time signatures and both swing and straight 8s feels. Try a slow 3/4 jazz waltz, or a fast funky 4/4.

Chapter summary

- Feel the *beat*: move and clap along, in a relaxed but controlled fashion, to a wide range of jazz.

- Hear the *pulse* of the music and tap the crotchets, minims and quavers.

- Develop your sense of pulse or *internal clock*. Practise with other musicians. Focus on listening and counting.

- Hear the different *feels* or subdivisions of the pulse, as either *swing*, where the pulse is broadly subdivided into three; or *straight*, where it is divided into two.

- Identify the various *grooves*—the rhythmic style or character of the music. Distinguish swing, rock and latin.

- Hear the *backbeat*, the stress on beats 2 and 4, in swing and rock grooves.

- Develop flexibility by practising *rhythmic placement*. Move simple rhythms through the bar in both swing and straight feels.

- Extend your improvising through *question and answer* techniques.

- Aim for a sound which is distinctive and improvise with musical character: explore dynamics, texture and levels of intensity; experiment with space; vary the tempo, time signature and feel.

Chapter 2   # Pitch

> Lee Morgan used to stand behind me when I was playing a
> ballad, and he'd be hollering, 'Play the pretty notes, man, play
> the pretty notes'. I thought I *was* playing the pretty notes but
> you know, things like that help you to reach a little further.
>
> GARY BARTZ

If you've worked through some of the activities in Chapter 1, you'll have begun to develop a strong sense of pulse, use simple rhythms with flexibility, accuracy and fluency, and invent short rhythmic phrases of your own. Now it's time to add pitch.

We begin by adding pitch to the question and answer activities explored in Chapter 1; we'll extend your rhythmic flexibility by reworking the rhythmic placement exercises, again with pitches added. We then look at ways you can accompany your early melodic improvisations and end by exploring pentatonic scales.

Always begin by keeping the range of choices narrow and using just a few pitches. It's important to gain confidence using a narrow range of pitches, before branching out to full scales. You'll soon discover that it is possible to make convincing musical sense and create variety with a small number of pitches, and many great jazz solos have grown from simple, restricted musical starting-points.

In the books of pieces you'll see this reflected in the guideline pitches suggested. As the grades progress, you'll notice a gradual increase in the number and range of pitches, from sets of two or three pitches at different parts of the scale, to whole pentatonic scales and other full scales and modes. You can of course add to these or choose different pitches if you want to, but begin by getting used to the discipline of working only with the given pitches, exploring fully the possibilities they offer.

Throughout, be vigilant about the rhythm skills already mastered. Once you move onto pitch, the rhythm may sometimes go soggy and boring while your attention is on another element. Continue to stretch yourself and strive for rhythmic invention, accuracy, flexibility and above all energy, because this is at the heart of all jazz playing, whatever the melodic and harmonic components are.

Question and answer

Let's begin by developing the question and answer activities we looked at in Chapter 1, this time playing a response on the piano.

One or two pitches

Limit yourself to one or two pitches to start with, using the second pitch to add colour and contrast. At this stage, it's worth imagining that you are playing two differently pitched drums for a rhythmic improvisation, rather than inventing a 'tune' in the conventional sense.

In the following examples we've chosen some pitches to start you off, taken from a single scale which we state below the example. As in the books of pieces, the pitches to improvise with are indicated in a guideline pitch box. Sing and play these guideline pitches before you begin to improvise, to get them into your ear.

Activities

1 Begin by playing the question, and then count the gap for the answer. Play the question several times, leaving the gap each time, until you can feel the length of the space.

♭3 pentatonic on G

2 Once you can do this, repeat the question again and again and copy it exactly, either by singing or playing or perhaps both.

3 Finally, begin to invent simple answers of your own to the question, choosing a couple of pitches from the note box. Here are a couple of examples:

4 Now try these activities with track 21, where we've extended our two-bar question into a twelve-bar blues. Count carefully throughout, and listen to the answers given, echo the question and give some answers of your own.

Limit your response to a couple of pitches so that you can concentrate on the rhythm as well, keeping this musical and stylish. Experiment with different pairs of notes from the note box: do some notes make the answer sound more 'finished' than others?

5 Now try the same activities with these questions, which use different feels and grooves. Choose only two pitches from the five given to start with.

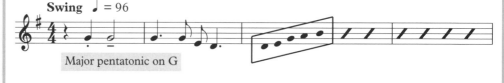

Major pentatonic on G

♭3 pentatonic on G

Dorian on D

6 These activities can be developed in all kinds of ways, leading to more fluent and inventive improvisations. Here are some suggestions:

(*a*) Force yourself to provide *different* answers each time. Concentrate first on one pitch and then another, perhaps using the second as a contrast only later in the phrase. Try starting your phrase on a different beat of the bar.

(*b*) Make *dynamic* changes. Follow a louder improvisation with a softer, perhaps less busy one.

(*c*) Try leaving a big gap at the start of one answer, and in the following one leave a big gap at the end. Next time, perhaps come straight in with a wallop and play throughout the entire length of the solo without stopping; the time after, place one or at the most two notes strategically and with great pride wherever you want, leaving a huge space around them.

(*d*) Vary the pitch of your two notes by going up or down an octave. How does this change the sound?

Three or four pitches

When you feel ready, go onto three or four pitches near to each other. Perhaps use the questions given above, or invent new ones of your own, as the basis of your work. You'll find many two-bar questions in the books of quick studies and aural tests published by the Board to accompany the jazz syllabus.

Even using three or four pitches, it's a useful rule of thumb not to use up all of your available musical resources straightaway. In this next example notice how only two pitches of the available four are used in the first few bars and how the addition of the other two later adds variety:

┌─ **Activities** ─────────────────────────────

As you begin to use more pitches, explore different activities to extend the range of your improvisation. Here are some suggestions:

1 Combine the technique of choosing one or two pitches at a time with a choice of dynamics or rhythmic shape. Use a variety of musical means to achieve your effect.

2 Try using two pitches for the question and another two for the answer:

3 Try repeating the same question round and round, choosing different numbers of pitches each time for your answer.

4 End your answers with different notes and consider which sounds more 'finished'. Compare these two answers:

The first answer, ending on the second note of the scale, sounds incomplete, and leads the ear back to the question. By contrast, the second answer, resolving onto the tonic or root, sounds complete, and ends the phrase in a satisfying way. It's important to signal the form in your improvising in ways like this, so that the structure is always clear.

5 Once you feel confident using more pitches, try one-bar questions and answers, and then make the space progressively longer, so that after regular practice your questions and answers are each lasting four bars each. Here is an example of a four-bar question:

Swing

♭3 pentatonic on C

6 Over time, you can begin to develop the question, as well as providing an answer to it, for example by varying it in some way or perhaps by leaving it out altogether and replacing it with a chord or other musical gesture.

Finally, you can begin to ask your own one-, two- or four-bar musical questions and answer them yourself. Suddenly, you are improvising whole phrases alone, unprompted by anything on the page!

Rhythmic placement

Look again at activity 5 above and notice how it begins on beat 2 of the bar. Jazz phrases can start on any beat or offbeat of the bar, so let's go back to the rhythmic placement exercises we did in Chapter 1, this time adding in pitches. Some of this may seem a little painstaking, particularly after you've been improvising two- or four-bar questions and answers. But these activities will make your melodies much more rhythmically flexible and allow you to improvise with much more confidence.

Individual notes

⌐ Activities ────────────────────────────────────

1   Begin by placing the note G on each beat of the bar in turn, exactly as you clapped the beats in Chapter 1:

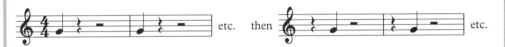

2   Now repeat the exercise, this time using two notes, G and B♭. Each time the beat to play on comes round, choose which note to play, for example:

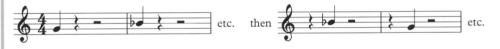

3   Try the same thing with groups of three notes, G, A and B♭, or perhaps D, E and G.

4   Now move on, as before, to placing individual pitches on each quaver too, in both 4/4 and 3/4. Practise in both straight and swing feels and at various speeds.

Common rhythms

⌐ Activities ────────────────────────────────────

1   Next, begin to move common melodic phrases through the bar, keeping the shape the same but moving the rhythm through the bar beat by beat, like this:

2 Now do the same thing again with a three-pitch phrase, like this:

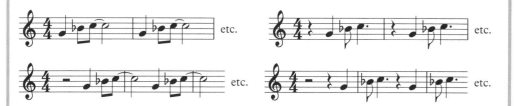

Be strict with yourself to begin with, and then, perhaps later on in the session, try the same thing again, but this time allow yourself a bit more freedom to work outside the strict repetition if you want to.

3 Another variant is to keep the rhythm the same each time and at the same point in the bar, but allow yourself to change the pitches, like this:

4 Finally, take a short rhythm and stick to it, but move it about the bar and use any of the available pitches, like this:

Hands together

You should now be able to improvise some reasonably inventive single-hand lines, and you've probably practised these in question and answer form with the CD tracks provided. You may know another player who could accompany you, but you'll soon want to provide your *own* accompaniments. A good starting-point is to use simple vamps or bass-lines.

Vamps and bass-lines

A vamp is a simple repeated figure, like an ostinato, used in swing and sometimes other styles. It can be played in the left hand alone or with both hands. Used as the basis for a whole accompaniment to a solo, it adds intensity to improvised sections. Each style has developed characteristic bass-lines, which, in their phrasing, rhythm and choice of notes, contribute to the groove.

Here are some examples of vamps which last for one or two bars, using a chord of G7:

Notice how the first two-bar vamp combines two of the one-bar vamps; you can use basic patterns such as these to create many different vamps.

Also try these vamps using these voicings for C7 and D7:

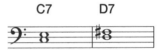

Here are some bass-lines:

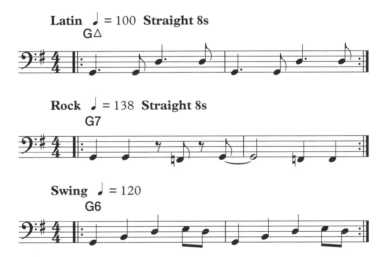

Play through these vamps and bass-lines and try them in different keys.

Activities

When you feel ready, try using a vamp to accompany question and answer phrases or some of the common melodic and rhythmic phrases you've been improvising with. Don't panic! Co-ordinating the hands can seem very difficult to begin with. Keep the vamp simple and work slowly.

1 Choose a one-bar vamp to begin with, and play it round several times in the left hand:

2 Add a right-hand part, keeping the rhythm constant and free of the rhythm of the vamp, and choosing simple melody notes. Perhaps something like this:

3 Now let the right-hand melody branch out a little, sometimes playing across the vamp and perhaps using more notes:

4 Make up a two-bar question with a vamp accompaniment and improvise answers to it. Perhaps start like this:

Initially your answer could be unaccompanied, with the vamp used just for the question. Later, try adding it to your answer as well.

From the start, try and invent vamps and bass-lines of your own to go with your own performances. They can add rhythmic tension to your solo, and, because they are repeated, they are sometimes easier to play than other kinds of accompaniment while improvising in the right hand.

Question and answer between the hands

Another way to accompany your own first attempts at improvising is to use your left hand to comment on your right, or vice versa. This could be as simple as leading with your left hand and following with your right:

Or you could lead with your right-hand melody and comment with a simple rhythmic phrase in your left:

Occasionally, you may want to bring both hands together for emphasis:

Keep the left hand *very* simple at the start, to keep the groove solid in the right.

As you can see, the hands do not need to play complex parts for the whole to sound satisfying and stylistic. This sort of question and answer, or leading and commenting, provides a structure for simple chords and pitches. As with so much in jazz, it's the rhythm of these phrases which makes the music interesting: the simple yet strong rhythms and occasional offbeat accents are enough to propel the music forward. Listen to track 25 and hear a twelve-bar blues using these various techniques.

Pentatonic scales

Let's now return to melodic work alone and look at whole pentatonic scales and areas within those scales. Many forms of the pentatonic or five-note scale are used in music from around the world. In the jazz syllabus, we've specified three forms: the major pentatonic, the ♭3 pentatonic and the minor pentatonic.

As you begin to use whole scales, guard against the danger of wandering up and down them aimlessly, without rhythmic focus or a sense of direction in the pitches used. Keep a sense of rhythmic vitality and work up to the full possibilities of the whole scale.

Major pentatonic

In jazz the most common pentatonic uses the 1st, 2nd, 3rd, 5th and 6th degrees of the major scale. Because it contains a major third, it is called the 'major pentatonic' in the jazz syllabus. Here are the major pentatonics beginning on C and G:

Activities

1   Divide up the scales into two halves, adding the first note again at the top. Play each half:

To begin with, use just these sets of notes in your improvising. Discover the various possibilities they contain: the bottom half contains stepwise movement only, while the top half introduces the characteristic gap of pentatonic scales.

2   Later try using the whole scale. Notice the gap appearing also between the third and fifth degrees. Try starting your improvisation on different notes of the scale and make up a simple vamp or bass-line to accompany your melody.

♭3 pentatonic

The ♭3 pentatonic scale is identical to the major pentatonic scale, except that the third note is flattened. This gives the scale a more 'bluesy' sound. Here are the ♭3 pentatonic scales on C and G:

This scale is extremely useful early on in learning to play jazz. You'll probably recognize it as the basis of some of the activities from earlier in this chapter and it's suggested as the basis for improvisation in a number of the early grade blues pieces in the graded albums.

Activities

1   As before, divide up the scale initially into two sets of three notes each, and explore different melodic shapes you can make, perhaps with a simple accompaniment.

2 Try inverting the notes of the scale, that is starting it on different notes. Here's the ♭3 pentatonic on G in root position and its four inversions:

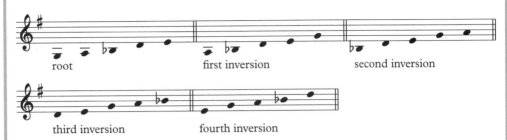

The third inversion is particularly useful for early melodic improvisation, because it falls neatly under the fingers.

Minor pentatonic

The minor pentatonic moves the gap to be between the 1st and 2nd notes and between the 4th and 5th. Its name derives from the interval of a minor 3rd between the first two notes. Here is the minor pentatonic on A:

Explore using this scale as you have done with the other pentatonic scales, and introduce it into your melodic improvising.

Chapter summary

○ Use *question and answer* activities to develop your melodic improvising. Begin with two pitches and later extend to three or four.

○ Be inventive in these activities: make dynamic changes, vary the pitch by an octave, explore the use of space, answer with just one or two notes strategically placed or with a flurry of quavers.

○ Practise with one-, two- and four-bar questions and answers, inventing some of your own.

○ Discover how ending with some pitches makes a phrase sound finished, while ending with others makes it sound more incomplete.

○ Use *rhythmic placement* activities to give your melodies rhythmic flexibility, starting with the placement of individual notes and extending this to short phrases.

○ Use simple *vamps* and *bass-lines* to accompany your melodic work. Develop your accompaniments using question and answer techniques.

○ Identify and use the *major, ♭3* and *minor pentatonic scales* to extend your melodic work. Try different inversions of the scales to create different melodic shapes.

Chapter 3 Introduction to Chords

> Everything that happened, happened by ear. For the two years I was with the band, we had a book of a hundred songs, and every one of us carried every last damn note of them in our heads.
>
> BILLIE HOLIDAY

The final element in this first three-stage package is the introduction of chords. We have left chords to the end because they can too easily become a major distraction, and concentrating too hard on getting the chords right can spoil all your good work on rhythmic accuracy, phrase length, melodic shape, dynamics and any other expressive function. Initially it is *much* more important to make rhythmic and melodic sense, and to keep the chords very simple.

Also, of course, the exam pieces *give* you the harmony, providing suitable left-hand chords to fit the tune. But later on you will often want to play jazz from a lead sheet which gives you only the melody and chord symbols, and so you'll have to create your own harmony. Or you might want to vary the left-hand chords we give and invent your own based on the harmony—the given chords are only a guideline, after all. In any event, understanding the chord symbols and the harmony of the tunes you play, especially common patterns like the twelve-bar blues and those of well-known standards, is essential to improvising well.

Chapters 3 and 4 set out the basics of jazz harmony, looking first at individual chords and then at simple, short chord sequences. You won't need all of the information shown here in order to get started, and indeed it is not assessed at all in the earlier grades. But once you have mastered simple rhythm and pitch improvising, you can begin to add the third dimension of chords to your awareness of the music, and this understanding of harmony will be necessary from Grade 4 onwards.

Always try to sing and then to play (in that order) the bass-lines and other pitches indicated—this will help get the sound of the chords and bass-lines into your ear from the very start. Then, as you learn a piece, extract individual chords, bass-lines and progressions from it and work on them in the ways shown in this chapter and the others that follow.

Degrees of the scale

To define what kind of a chord we are using, we often refer to the *degrees* of a scale, for example, the 1st, 3rd and 5th. These are simply the names given to the particular pitches which sit a certain number of notes away from the root in the mode. So if C is note 1 in the scale, the 3rd of the major scale of C is three notes up from C, the note E.

Activities

Learning to pitch intervals will help you greatly to identify chords. Practise identifying pitches with the numbers to make intervals and then short melodies. If you're familiar with sol-fa, you could also use this to identify the pitches.

1   Begin with the first three degrees of the scale, singing 1, 2 and 3, like this:

and then making up pitch combinations to remember. For example, sing 3–1:

or 1–2

or any of these patterns:

   1–3, 1–2–1, 1–3–1, 2–3–1, 1–3–2–1, and so on.

Sing them only when you can pitch each note in your head before you sing it. Check yourself on the piano if necessary to see if you are right in each case.

   Finally, choose a number combination, sing it, and then play it on the piano, like this:

think: sing: play:

3–2–1

2   Once you can hear, sing and play notes 1–3, add notes 4 and 5. Try pitching, singing and playing these melodic fragments in just the same way as before:

   1–5–1, 1–3–5, 1–2–5–1, 5– 4–3– 4–5, 5–3–2–3–5.

3   Once this is secure, focus on the group of notes at the top of the scale: 5, 6, 7 and the higher 1 too.

4   There are other activities you can do, for example:
     (*a*) singing a phrase and then working out the degrees of the scale it uses;
     (*b*) singing a phrase and then playing it direct, visualizing the degrees of the scale in your head.

Neither of these is as hard as it sounds if you limit the number of available pitches at the start!

5 Once you've mastered this in C major, try doing the same exercises with Dorian on D and Mixolydian on G. Listen to how the 3rd and 7th degrees of the scale vary compared with C major.

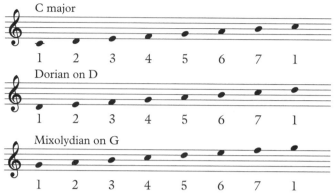

6 Now turn to a piece you are learning and sing the degrees of the scale from the solo section. Find the root in the bass and then number each note as you sing it.

Chords

A chord is simply two or more notes played at the same time. To begin with you will be using two-, three- and sometimes four-note chords, but chords can eventually contain as many notes as you want.

This section shows you how to label chords using *symbols* and *Roman numerals*. The symbols are explained in the text. Roman numerals are simply another means of identifying a chord and take their name from the note on which the chord is based. So note 1 in C major is C, and chord I in C major is the chord built on C. The different ways these systems are used will be explained at the end of the chapter.

The root

At the bottom of every (root-position) chord is its root. If you are asked to identify the root of a chord, always listen for the lowest note you can hear.

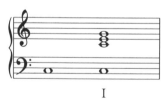

─ Activities ─

1 Listen for and sing back the roots of the following individual chords:

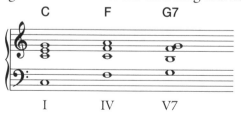

2 Now listen for the roots moving in these simple repeating chord sequences containing two and then four chords:

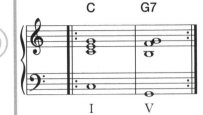 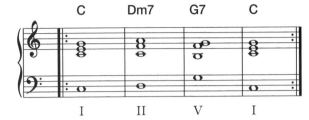

Sing the roots back to yourself until you can hear them accurately at the bottom of the texture—think of them as a melody if that helps.

3 Repeat the chords and sing or play a simple melody over the top, using the notes C, D, E and G. Listen for the bass-line.

This succession of roots, the root movement, is the **bass-line** of the chord sequence. The roots of each chord follow each other in a low but very important melody which provides the backbone to the chord sequence of a piece.

When jazz musicians say they 'know' a tune, they mean they can sing back and play by heart not only the top line melody, but also the root movements of the chord sequence. Both of these are essential for successful improvising. As they improvise, experienced jazz musicians follow the chord sequence in their heads by singing or playing the roots to themselves. As a bass-player improvises a bass-line, he or she will use the roots of the chord sequence as a guide, and any other soloist must also take account of the harmony in choosing which notes to play.

Once you get more advanced you will be able to do this yourself in your head too, but to begin with, simply singing the bass-lines of the tunes you are learning, out loud, along to the CD or even a recording of yourself playing them, will be sufficient. If it helps, use the chord symbols written above the solo section to help you, or, if you read stave notation, read the left-hand figurations given.

The 3rd

Counting up from the root, we have already seen that the 3rd of the chord sits on the 3rd degree of the scale. So if the note C is your root (note 1), the 3rd will be some kind of E:

From G, the 3rd will be some sort of B. Listen to the gap of one note between root and 3rd and sing it back.

The 3rd can be raised or lowered. The raised 3rd is known as the **major 3rd**, and the lowered 3rd as the **minor 3rd**. As with classical music, a major chord is a chord containing a major 3rd between root and third, and a minor chord is a chord containing a minor 3rd between root and 3rd.

In jazz a chord of C major is written simply as 'C' and a chord of G major as 'G':

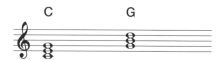

A minor chord is indicated using the symbol 'm', so a chord of C minor is 'Cm' and a chord of G minor 'Gm':*

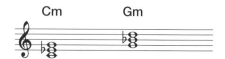

Activities

1 Sing and then play both E and E♭ against C and get used to the darker sound that a minor 3rd makes against its root.

2 Sing the chord sequence I–II–V–I again, this time adding the 3rd to your root, as follows:

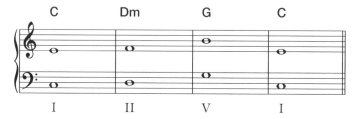

3 Now repeat this in G:

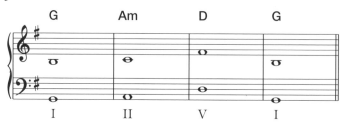

4 Sing and then play the 3rds in your chords. Which are major and which are minor?

The 5th

The 5th of the chord sits five notes up from the root on the 5th degree of the scale—for example, a 5th above C is the note G. Play both these notes separately and together and listen to the sound.

Activities

1 Sing and play through the chord sequence I–II–V–I, this time adding the 5th to your root and 3rd:

---

* A minus sign is also used in jazz to indicate a minor chord, but throughout the Board's publications we've used 'm' to avoid any confusion between a minus sign and ledger line.

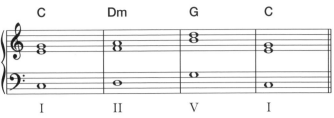

2 Now listen to track 28 and hear the 3rd and then the 5th against the I–II–V–I root.

3 Look at a piece you are learning, and find and then sing and play the fifth of each chord.

The triad

Adding the root, 3rd and 5th together gives us the **triad**, the most basic form of chord. Here are the triads of C major and C minor—notice how the E moves but the G stays the same:

Sing these two triads on C, note by note, and then play them.

Activities

1 Work out major and minor triads starting on other roots. Sing the notes of the triad in each case. Notice how they sometimes include sharps and flats, and involve different hand shapes.

2 Play major and minor triads at different parts of the piano. Double up some of the notes. Space the notes in different ways. How does the sound vary? Which chord spacing sounds best? The different spacings of chords are called voicings—more about this later.

3 Play through the I–II–V–I chord sequence again, this time playing triads above each of the bass notes, like this:

For completeness, let us now build a triad on every degree of the scale of C, one by one, using all the white notes, as follows:*

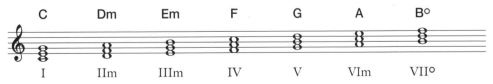

*A detailed knowledge of *all* these is not required at this stage.

These triads are all *diatonic* to the major scale, that is to say they are made up exclusively with notes from that scale and will sound good with it. Chords I, IV and V are major and are sometimes called the 'primary triads'; these chords alone are used in the simplest twelve-bar blues. Chords II, III and VI are minor; these are sometimes called the 'secondary triads'.

You will see that we can also name *chords* using the Roman numeral of the degree of the scale on which they sit. So, for example, in C major the chord of C is also known as chord I, D as chord II, G as chord V and so on. We can add 'm' where necessary to indicate minor. The final chord, based on B, contains a diminished 5th, which is indicated by a circle. We'll come to this chord in Part II.

Using triads to make melodies

One way to improvise over chords is to play up and down the tones of a triad. In some of the earlier styles of jazz, such as ragtime and what is known as New Orleans jazz, the basic triad tones, as they are called, still play a particularly important part in the improvising. The calypso 'Becky's Song', from the book of Grade 2 pieces, also uses triad tones in the head and as the basis for improvisation. See some other examples on p. 50.

However, if you only learn to play in this way, the result can lack smoothness, and be jerky and unmelodic, creating a series of arpeggio fanfares above the chords. Good improvising involves making many different kinds of melodies over the changing harmony, and triad shapes are only one type of melodic shape among many possibilities, including stepwise movement in scales and much wider leaps than 3rds and 5ths. At the start, it is best to choose a cluster of notes near each other and to relate your improvising to portions of scales, such as those given in the books of pieces.

The 7th

After the triad, we come to the 7th. To sing the 7th degree of the scale, sing up the scale from the root to the 7th note:

or sing down one note in the mode from the root:

Triads are not the only chord used in jazz. In many jazz chords musicians use the 7th as a normal addition to or a replacement for the 5th, because it makes the sound richer. So unlike classical music, many jazz chords contain three notes: the root, 3rd and 7th, like this:

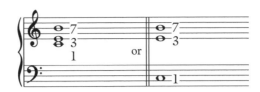

or four notes, the root, 3rd, 5th and 7th, like this:

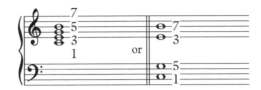

If they only contain three notes they often contain the root, 3rd and *7th*, rather than the root, 3rd and *5th*. Here is the chord again in a more common voicing in the style, omitting the 5th:

The seven (7) chord and major seven (△) chord

Like the 3rd, the 7th degree of the scale has two possible positions, each of which gives a different colour to a chord containing it. In a chord, the 7th may be *raised* (major 7) or *lowered* (7), like this:

What classical musicians would call a dominant 7th (or sometimes the interval of a minor 7th above the root), for example B♭ over a C root, is in jazz stated in the chord name simply as the '7', as follows:

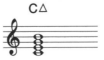

A **major 7th**, B♮ over a C root, is stated in the chord name as a 'major 7', written as 'maj7' or with a triangle, as follows:

This is called a chord of Cmaj7.

1 Play the chords of C, G, F and D with added 7ths, as C7, G7, F7 and D7:

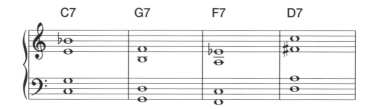

2 Now play them with major 7ths, as CΔ, GΔ, FΔ and DΔ:

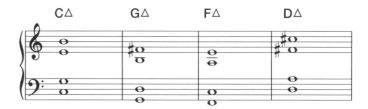

Listen to the way the sound changes and sing up the triad to the 7th in each case.

3 Try singing and then playing the 7th or major 7th in each of the following chords. In the first set the 7th degree is at the top of the texture, whereas in the second it is in other positions in the chord, making it slightly harder to identify:

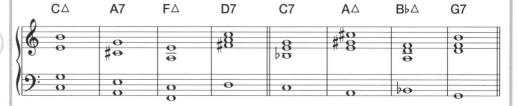

4 Play through this example and listen for the different 7ths. Sing and play them separately against the root.

Straight 8s Latin

etc.

5 Play each of the following chords and identify whether each is a major 7th or a 7th by singing up from the root:

6   Now choose a particular note—root, 3rd, 5th or 7th—and try to sing and then play the chosen degree in the chords you've just played and listened to.

7   Finally, try singing and playing the 3rd and either the major 7th or 7th above these bass notes:

The minor seven (m7) chord and minor major seven (m△) chord

Both the seven chord and major seven chord contain a major 3rd. What 7th chords do we get if we use a *minor* 3rd?

Let's take a minor triad, for example C minor (i); then add to it a 7th to make a **minor seven chord**, in this case C minor 7 or Cm7 (ii); then add a *major* 7th to the triad, making a **minor major seven chord**, in this case C minor major 7, or Cm△ (iii):

Play these chords and listen to their different sounds, singing all the pitches.*

Activities

1   Now go through the same activities we did for the 7th and major 7th, but this time also identifying the 3rd too. Sing up the root, 3rd, 5th and 7th degrees of each of these chords. Focus first on the 3rd—is it major or minor?—and then on the 7th—is it a major 7th or a 7th?

30

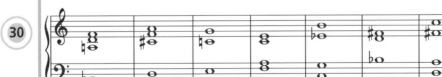

---

* Until you become familiar with the names of these sounds, you may find it useful to insert a comma between the different elements to indicate which part of the chord symbol refers to the 3rd and which to the 7th, like this:

C minor, 7   C, 7
C minor, major 7   C, major 7

2 Now take a series of different roots and sing first a minor 3rd and then a major 3rd above each. Next sing a 7th and then a major 7th.

The sus4

There is an extra position that the 3rd of a triad sometimes takes up, and that is the **sus4** or suspended 4th:

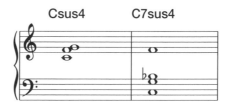

Sometimes these chord symbols are simplified to 'Csus' and 'C7sus', and this is the way we have written them in the books of pieces.

The sus4 is a more dissonant and unstable sound and often feels as though it wants to resolve down to the 3rd:

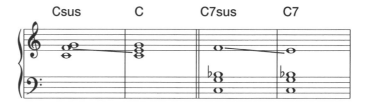

At other times it is used as a colour in its own right.

We can summarize all these chords on a table, representing the five different possible chords of C like this:

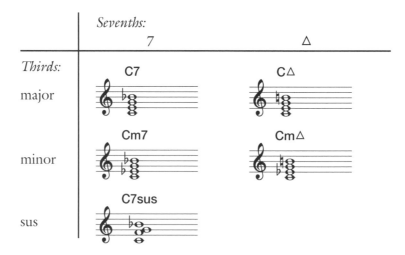

These five basic chords are the commonest chords of jazz harmony. Sing all the notes in each chord and practise playing each of them on each of the roots given in the scale syllabus. Get to know their sound and find examples of them in the pieces you are playing.

Voicings

In the examples of chords given in this chapter, we've tended to give the chord in full (sometimes in a form for right hand alone, sometimes split between the hands), so that the form of the chord and the notes it contains are clear. However, it is very definitely *not* a good idea to play chords in this way—the effect would be very stodgy and unstylish!

Most of the time jazz musicians do not play all the notes of the chord. They choose particular combinations of notes to create the sound they want, and these sounds are called **voicings**. Full 7th chords can be reduced to just two notes to create very characteristic sounds and textures of great clarity. There are many examples of this in the early grade pieces.

There are many different voicings for each chord. To begin with, you will generally only need to play voicings containing two notes for Grades 1 and 2, usually consisting of (i) the root and 3rd; (ii) the root and 7th; or (iii) the 3rd and 7th:

Playing two-note voicings throughout keeps the texture even. Notice how the voicings in the early grade pieces have been chosen to minimize the movement in your left hand. This helps keep the voice-leading smooth.

As your confidence increases, sometimes you may also like to use full 1, 3, 5 triads, 1, 3, 7 voicings, or just the root itself, depending on the context and your own taste. Keep it simple and avoid clogging the texture by playing every note. As with so much, less is more.

Activities

1 Practise voicing common chords like C7, F7, G7 and D7 in different ways, for example using the root and 3rd, the root and 7th, 3rd and 7th or the root and 5th. In the grade pieces you will find it helpful to follow the given guideline voicings to begin with. But you will soon get used to the shapes, and want to experiment with other voicings of your own.

Chord symbols and Roman numerals

We've looked at the common chords of jazz and voiced them in different ways. Let's look again at the two systems of notation used to identify chords and consider the information they give.

Chord symbols

Chord symbols are found in most notated jazz music, sometimes written above and sometimes in the middle of the stave, depending on the publisher (we've put them above the stave). They indicate the harmonic background to the music, the chords that are to be played and the underlying movement of the harmony, by showing the positions of each note within the chord—for example that a 7th chord contains the root, 3rd, 5th and 7th, and what kind of 3rd and 7th each is. The symbols indicate a particular set of notes; they show the *vertical* perspective of each chord.

Roman numerals

We began by seeing the Roman numeral as a way of defining which degree of a scale a particular note was on. We then saw how a numeral defines a chord, by indicating the triad on a particular degree of the scale, and how it sits in relation to the home chord. This gives each chord a particular function within the sequence, or, if you like, its *horizontal* perspective.

Where does a chord sit in relation to the home key? Is it 'tense' (a chord V, for example) or 'resolved' (a chord I) in that place in the piece? This information is given by the Roman numeral, which when shown is usually written under the chord. As with chord symbols, the Roman numeral system also shows that a chord is either major (no symbol) or minor (add m), and contains either a major 7 (add Δ) or a 7 (add 7).

Roman numerals replace specific roots in the notation and indicate the relationship within the key, but not the key itself. Unlike chord symbols, they do not of themselves indicate particular pitches until a key is added.

So a 'II–V–I' progression, which we cover in the next chapter, is actually shorthand for the chords IIm7, V7, IΔ, and this progression then occurs in a particular key, for example in C major as this:

Dm7   G7   CΔ

Or in G major as this:

Am7   D7   GΔ

This is the same progression, using the same key relationships (shown by the Roman numerals), but in a different key. Dm7 is acting as chord II in C major, and Am7 is acting as chord II in G major.

Chapter summary

○ Familiarize yourself with the *degrees* of the scale, for example the 3rd and 5th.

○ Listen for and sing the *roots* or lowest notes of simple chords.

○ Learn to identify *major 3rds* and *minor 3rds*.

○ Add the *5th* to root and 3rd to form *triads*.

○ Learn to sing and play the *7th* of a chord.

○ Practise playing and identifying the *various 7 chords*: the seven chord; the major seven chord; the minor seven chord; the minor major seven chord.

○ Find the final position the 3rd sometimes occupies in a triad: the *sus4*.

○ Find and use the common two-note voicings of 7, Δ, m7 and mΔ chords. Try different spacings, adding or leaving out some of the notes of a chord to see what effect this has.

○ Learn to identify chords by the *chord symbols* used; practise also naming chords using *Roman numerals*.

Chapter 4

Using Chords in Chord Sequences

You're never in a secure position. You're never at a point where you have it all sewn up. You have to choose to be secure like a stone, or insecure but able to flow.

KEITH JARRETT

Generally, improvisation takes place over a string of chords, which we call the changes. The II–V–I is one such example. An awareness of the shape of a tune's chord sequence is fundamental to improvising successfully.

In the band the changes are realized by the rhythm section (drums, bass and piano or guitar), which makes a background harmonic and rhythmic texture, a kind of scaffolding which the improvising musician embellishes and interacts with. Sometimes there may be only one or two changes over a sixteen-bar sequence, creating a sense of open space in the harmonic texture. In other tunes, the harmony can move from one change to the next twice or even four times a bar.

Chord sequences are often notated by writing the changes above the stave with diagonal slashes in the stave to indicate that the soloist is to improvise at this point, something like this:

Often there is one slash per beat (in this case 4 slashes per bar). The soloist invents a left-hand part that realizes the chords given and improvises melodies over the chord in the right hand.

Let's begin by looking at the simplest and most commonly used progressions one by one.

The twelve-bar blues

The twelve-bar blues is one of the most popular and often played forms used in mainstream jazz. The sequence in all its variants appears in many other related but distinct styles, including the more guitar-based Rhythm and Blues (R'n'B) tradition, from which many styles of rock music emerged. The boogie-woogie styles of the 1910s and 1920s contain twelve-bar blues chord sequences and vocabulary similar to what later became rock-n-roll piano. In the bebop style of the 1940s and 1950s, different chords are substituted—we'll look at these in a later chapter. There are also blues sequences that are longer and shorter than twelve bars. But at Grades 1–5 we will be focusing on the ways in which the twelve-bar blues has been used and developed in jazz.

The form of the twelve-bar blues

In its simplest form the twelve-bar blues is a short, repeated chord sequence lasting twelve bars, made with just three chords built on the root, 4th and 5th of the scale. Here are the three chords in G major:

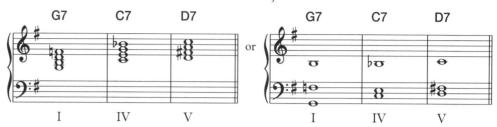

The whole twelve-bar blues sequence looks like this:

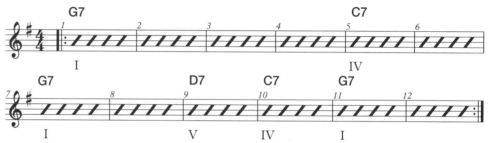

The first chord (G7, chord I), lasts for four bars, the next chord (C7, chord IV) for two, and the next (G7) for two. Then chords V and IV (D7 and C7) last for one bar each, and the final chord I lasts for two bars.

It is important to count this form out accurately, so you know where you are in the sequence. You may find it helpful to think of the sequence as three lots of four bars to begin with, and then to divide each four-bar block into a question and then an answer lasting two bars each.

A useful exercise is to play through the sequence several times on the piano and record yourself. When you play back the tape, stop at particular moments and ask yourself which bar of the sequence you are on. If you have a friend or teacher to help you, get them to play it and test you until you can tell which bar is which in the sequence by ear.

Learning the twelve-bar blues

Activities

The twelve-bar blues is such an important sequence, you must learn it thoroughly. Here's how to do it:

1   Set your metronome at around crotchet = 108 and sing and play through the bass-line alone until you can do it by heart:

Tap the beats of the bar and move to the new notes on the first beat of the bar clearly and positively.

2   Now add the 3rd, singing and then playing through the sequence:

Try and keep the root in your head, even when you are singing the 3rd, so that the root movement is always clear in your mind whatever other pitches you may be singing or playing.

3   Now add the 5th. Keep the beat going and feel the movement to the different chords.

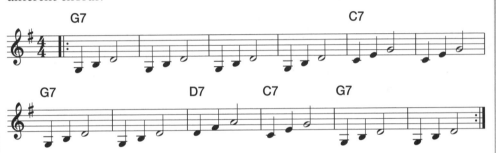

4   Finally, add the 7th. Singing this may be tricky at first, but persevere! Playing these broken chords on the piano is a lot easier.

5   Try playing the broken chords of the last example down an octave in the left-hand and make up some right-hand chord patterns to play above. You could begin like this:

This twelve-bar blues sequence should be firmly in your mind by now.

6   Learn to play the blues in other keys. Here is the bass-line for the sequence in C, introducing a characteristic variant in bar 12 (chord V):

Listen to track 31 and hear the trio play this sequence in C, with the pianist building from root, to 3rd, to 5th and then 7th.

7   Now listen to track 32 on the CD, and hear the trio improvising on a twelve-bar blues in G. Hear first the bass-player plucking the roots alone, exactly as you did to start with. Then hear him invent a walking bass to *embellish* these roots. Hear how he plays the other chord tones (3rd, 5th and 7th) and other passing notes to create smooth or leaping lines around the harmonic framework.

In the third chorus, the pianist joins in, inverting suitable chord voicings and melody lines to interact with the bass-player. Finally the drummer adds patterns to the texture. It may sound complex and free, but underneath is a solid statement of the twelve-bar blues in G, exactly as you've learnt to play yourself.

The II–V–I

After the twelve-bar blues, the II–V–I is one of the most common chord progressions, not just in jazz but across many styles of tonal music. It is found particularly in bebop 1940s and 1950s jazz. The name derives from chords II and V, which precede chord I at the cadence. Here is an example in C major:

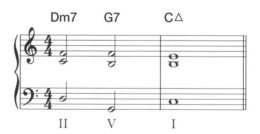

Notice how, in a major key, chord II is always a minor 7 chord, chord V is always a 7 chord, acting as a dominant, and chord I is always a maj7 chord. Now play these yourself as broken chords, like this:

Guide tones

Look again at the chords in the above example. Each of the three chords—Dm7, G7, C△—is made up of the root, 3rd and 7th. The 3rd and 7th are called the **guide tones** (or sometimes the tendency tones), because they 'guide' the harmony. The movement of these guide tones away from and towards points of rest creates the feeling of forward motion typical of jazz cadential harmony.

We'll come to how they do this in a minute. But for the moment, note that in mainstream jazz, pianists often base their voicings on the guide tones and omit the 5th, because using the guide tones is the simplest way of delineating the movement of the harmony within the sequence. For this reason, and also because they are relatively easy to play and make good **inner lines**, playing the guide tones is a good place to begin when realizing jazz chord sequences.

Tension and release

So how do these guide tones work?

When we looked at how Roman numerals indicate the horizontal perspective of the harmony, we spoke of chords being 'tense' or 'resolved' within a harmonic progression. Some chords seem more 'unstable' or tense than others, because they seem to want the music to continue or resolve to a chord which is more stable.

Activities

1   Play a well-known phrase such as the opening of 'Three Blind Mice' and stop on 'blind':

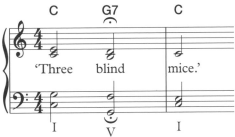

This feels unfinished, because the notes of the G7 chord need to resolve to the C chord. The 7th of the G7 chord (the F) is dissonant with the G and is pulled down to the E of the C major chord, while the 3rd of the G7 chord (the B) is the leading note of C major and tends to resolve to a C.

These are our guide tones in action. The 3rd and 7th of the G7 chord are 'guiding' the harmony forwards, to resolution on C.

2   Now sing each of the parts in this same V–I progression. Sing first the bass-line, G moving to C; then the leading note resolving, B moving to C; and finally the F moving down to the E:

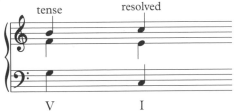

3 Play these same chords in their more common jazz form:

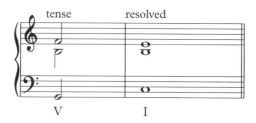

Notice that chord I contains a major 7th (the note B) yet this remains a resolved chord. The maj7 is used so commonly in jazz that it is part of the *colour* of chord I. The ear accepts the B as part of the C major chord and not as a dissonant note requiring resolution. (Notice also that chord I may be C7 too.)

4 Add chord II before this V–I cadence (to complete the II–V–I progression) and see the guide tones of chord II working in a similar fashion:

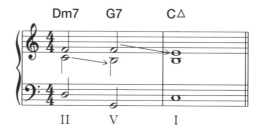

5 Sing and play the separate lines over the root:

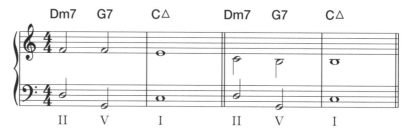

The 7th of Dm7 (the C) is dissonant with the root (the D) and needs to resolve to the B of the G7 chord. The 3rd of the Dm7 chord (the F) sits 'waiting' to become the 7th of the G7 chord.

Inner lines

Look again at the II–V–I progression and notice the smoothness of the lines made by the 3rds and 7ths:

The root moves in large leaps, but the chords themselves stay in the same register and texture. There are two lines at work here in the top stave, one where the F moves to the E and one connecting the C with the B. This voicing makes clear lines and is more satisfactory on the ear than, for example:

The 3rds and 7ths, when put in strings of chords, create a series of long inner lines. They create a jazz counterpoint where lines move against each other in similar and contrary motion, exactly the same as in classical harmony and obeying the same harmonic 'rules'.

These inner lines can be contained in the melody in many different ways, each a good expression of the harmonic movement. An improviser could produce melodies which articulate the movement of these inner lines (the first four bars of the next example), or complement the movement of the inner lines by playing around them and using other related notes (the second four bars):

In each case, notice how you can *hear* the chords in the melody played.

Activities

1 Play the II–V–I sequence in F, G and Bb. Notice the movement of the inner lines and make up simple melodies based on these, some which articulate and follow the movement of the lines, and some which play against this movement.

2 Play through the twelve-bar blues in C and in G using guide tones in the right hand and roots in the left, and note the way the inner lines work. In C, you'll use sequences like these:

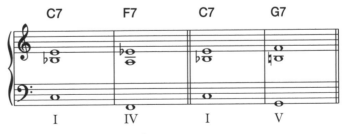

3 Find examples of these guide tones in blues pieces from the books of pieces (examples are 'Bags' Groove' at Grade 1 and 'Good Time Blues' at Grade 2).

Other common chord progressions

Working with common chord progressions of two, three or four chords each is the best way to prepare to play over standards. Here are some examples and some activities to practise them.

Activities

1 Play this progression using I, IV, V, I:

2 Reinforce the harmony in your ear. First sing the bass-line of the progression in semibreves (C–F–G–C), and then sing and play broken-chord patterns based on the triads, first simply and then with more rhythmic interest:

3 Experiment with different melody lines. Here's one where the hand moves less:

4 Use this progression as the basis for a left-hand pattern, playing some simple voicings or improvising a melody with the right hand. Try altering the texture to include left-hand two- or three-note voicings (including 7ths). Extend the exercise further by using a variety of grooves and metres, playing at different speeds and practising in a number of keys. Finally, relate this to a real tune by finding one where this progression occurs and playing it.

Notice in the above example the voicings given in the right hand. The minimum movement allows the hand to stay in the same position—for the first two chords, for example, the thumb stays on C, even though the chord changes from C to F. These voicings also create smooth melodic lines: G–A–B–G; E–F–G–E; C–C–D–C. The important principle is: never move your hand further than necessary when changing chords and move to the nearest note where possible. This makes for physical efficiency and also creates a smooth and even sound.

A great many standards are constructed from a limited number of common progressions. Below are some standard major key progressions; by each one is the name of a standard for you to find that uses this progression.

Roman Numerals	In C	Other Keys	Standards
I–V–I	C–G–C	(E♭) E♭–B♭–E♭	'Ice Cream' (Kid Ory)
I–IV–V–I	C–F–G–C	(A) A–D–E–A	many calypsos
I–II–V–I	C–Dm–G–C	(B♭) B♭–Cm–F–B♭	'Somebody loves me' (Gershwin)
‖: I–VI–II–V :‖	C–Am–Dm–G	(F) F–Dm–Gm–C	'I Got Rhythm' (Gershwin)
‖: I–II–III–IV :‖	C–Dm–Em–F	(G) G–Am–Bm–C	'Autumn in New York' (Vernon Duke)
‖: I–IV–III–II :‖	C–F–Em–Dm	(D) D–G–F♯m–Em	'We're a couple of swells' (Berlin)

Activities

1 Play these progressions using triad voicings and then 137 voicings. Sing the bass-line and then the inner parts one by one.

2 Learn each in C major and then in at least one other key as shown (learning in another key reinforces the progression in your mind and makes you more flexible).

3 Write each one out on manuscript paper. Voice each sequence in your left hand and invent a short improvisation in your right, for example:

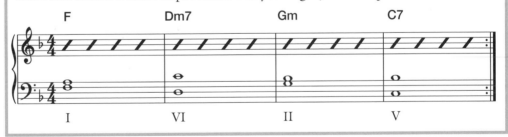

You will find many of these progressions in the books of jazz piano pieces. Quite a few tunes are also built up from a simple repeating bass-line, and these are also useful for identifying cadences and harmonic movement. Some famous examples of this are from the work of the South African pianist Abdullah Ibrahim, previously known as Dollar Brand, who has written many simple but effective tunes from repeated bass-lines using common chords. The best way to learn is by applying small quantities at a time to a piece you are learning.

Once you can sing the bass-line and the inner lines in your head by heart and can predict where they move, your solos will soon take on a new confidence and freedom. It is only through an aural understanding of how the chords function that you can really hold your head up and say 'I know this tune!'

Chapter summary

○ Learn to play the *twelve-bar blues*.

○ Learn to play the *II–V–I* in various common keys and find examples in the pieces you are learning.

○ Identify the *guide tones* guiding the harmony in a II–V–I, and sing the smooth progression of the *inner lines*.

○ Play other simple common chord progressions and find examples of them in your pieces. Become familiar with their voicings and invent improvisations over them.

Chapter 5   # Doodling

But then again, you can do what the hell you like . . .

EDDIE HARVEY

We've looked at specific areas of jazz piano in turn; now it's time to look at the big picture and start doodling.

In the early to mid 1960s, jazz musicians like saxophonist Ornette Coleman, bass-player Charles Mingus and pianist Cecil Taylor invented new ways of playing which aimed for a new freedom. It is to these kinds of playing that we now turn.

For those beginning to play jazz, free improvising is particularly useful as a balance to more detailed work. It relies more on emotion, mood, atmosphere and intuition, or painting a picture. It is a good way of learning to get ideas flowing, and then channelling that flow once it begins. It helps get rid of inhibitions and builds confidence in a player. It also helps you learn to enjoy the sound of the instrument for its own sake, and experience the joy of creative and emotional freedom that comes from improvising.

Activities

1   *Get the flow going*   Start by just doodling at the keyboard for say 10–30 seconds. Play literally anything, until you come up with an idea that you could develop—perhaps a basic rhythm, a fragment of melody or an unusual sonority. Play with the sounds of the piano in a childlike way, for sheer enjoyment.

Now stop, and repeat what you have. Focus on stating a single idea of your own, clearly and accurately, perhaps for just four bars. Try to sing the idea in your head before you play it. It may change when you come to play it, but at least you will have established the mood in your mind.

Do you have a clear idea of what you might play next? The idea is to get the flow going and then stop. Think of the first two bars of a tune—its groove, its character, its hook or opening. Play it, get the music flowing and then stop as soon as you know what would happen next. Do another totally different one straight away. You could perhaps use a piece you are playing to start you off.

 Some starting-points are demonstrated on track 34.

2   *Deciding when to stop*   Now continue one or two of the ideas, perhaps using question and answer, simple repetition, or continuing with another different idea. If you are working alone, record yourself, listen back and be critical. Did it go on too long? How long can you sustain a single idea? How can you end? What should happen next? Try again with something completely different.

When you can get a flow of music going and can decide when and how to stop, have a go at each of the following activities, in any order. Just launch in without preparation and see what you get! You'll be surprised at how coherent and meaningful a short free improvisation can be, even at the beginning. Anything you play can lead you suddenly to explore – a texture, a note cluster or a few pecks at the keyboard; anything might spark a more fully formed idea. Remember that with all these activities there are no right answers – *you* are setting the structure and taking the decisions. But be critical – try each several times and improve it as you go.

Some definite starting-points

Choose any three pitches, within the range of a 5th, say, or an octave, or three octaves. Play a repeated pattern of one or two bars using only these three pitches. Fix one area of your playing but allow freedom in other respects, for example:

- Try using a pre-set rhythm but any pitches
- or pre-set pitches but any rhythm
- play a fixed chord but with no pulse
- keep to a given rhythm but vary the range of dynamics, or the register of the keyboard
- explore different textures: two part, unaccompanied right-hand melody, bass-line and chords, chords and melody, chords across two hands.

Emulate another player

Listen carefully to about 10 or 20 seconds of an improvisation by an established player. Try to describe in words what was going on and why you liked it. Concentrate on one particular aspect: the rhythms, use of tempo, melodic lines, chord shapes, form, the pace of the solo, texture of sound, touch, phrase lengths, dynamic contrasts, and so on.

Now emulate by ear one aspect of that performance in a short free improvisation. You might, for instance, be copying the use of quiet, still chords; space and silence in phrases; stabby, exciting textures; flowing lines. See whether you can move from quiet to loud over the same period. Aim to capture the overall feeling or mood at the early stages rather than specific notes. Try several times, thinking about problems and possible solutions between each attempt. Work directly from recordings.

Vaguer exploration

Play anything at all for around a minute. Play until you find a repeated pattern you like. Stop and investigate it. Play it repeatedly until you think of a second line to play with the other hand. As far as possible, be guided by your ear and intuition, and not by your hand. If it helps, sing the second line before you play it.

Different rhythmic styles and time signatures

Make up your own vamp or rhythm, or choose one from a recording that you like. Try playing the vamp at different speeds, in swing or straight feel. Add or take away a beat, so that 3/4 becomes 4/4 or 4/4 becomes 3/4. Play different patterns or lines above the vamp. Ornament the bass-line by adding notes of the scale or chromatic notes outside it. Alter the pitches to make it more stepwise or more jagged.

Invent little melodies over the vamp, perhaps only two or four bars long at first. Think how you could develop these in various ways. Perhaps you could play the vamp through a chord sequence, or continue the melody by repeating it at a different pitch or with a new contrasting section.

Sonorities

Try playing block chords of three or four notes in the middle register and then higher up or lower down. What difference does this make to the sound of the chords? Play very beautifully.

Try playing a melody over a single line bass-line. Play these lines in different registers: the bass-line low down and the melody in the top octave; the hands closer together in the middle of the keyboard. How could you use these sounds in your solos or head arrangements?

Exploring extremes

Play as softly as you can for ten seconds and then as loudly as you can for five. Try a furious burst of fast notes, and then play quiet, peaceful chords. Play only in the top octave of your instrument. Improvise in more extreme registers than usual: up or down an octave, two octaves, or jumping from one end to the other. Play with your right hand in registers below middle C. If it helps, think of a story, like a chase in a Tom and Jerry cartoon!

Two parts

Choose one note in your left hand as a drone (a fixed note that will not change) and a second note in your right hand. Play them together, as a performance. With no pulse, now choose with great care and solemnity another single note to follow the first right-hand note, playing that note also against the drone. Listen carefully to the contrast between these two musical events. Repeat the exercise using different right-hand notes to create a variety of effects.

Next, try the same exercise, choosing a series of three to five different long notes in the right hand against this fixed note in the left hand, to make a short, intense melody. Are the notes you choose going to be near each other or far apart? Are they going to be loud or soft? Do all notes sound the same against the fixed note? Try ones very close to the given one, and ones far apart from it. Play each note in turn, restriking the drone each time as you do so. Now extend it as long as you want, but make sure you choose every note carefully. Try and sing each note before you play it. Perhaps embellish the movement between notes.

Repeat this exercise again, this time keeping the *right* hand on a single fixed pitch (perhaps punctuated with some movement), and varying the left hand to make a moving bass-line.

Finally try moving both at the same time.

If you want to introduce a pulse, or repeat a sequence of notes in the left hand, do so. But remember to choose every note carefully.

Musicians in the 1960s used techniques like these to achieve a new freedom in jazz. Avoiding pre-set structural principles such as harmony, form and rhythmic style, they experimented with using two rhythm sections at once, renouncing the use of triads and tonal harmony, widening the range of instruments and playing for indeterminate lengths of time. Keith Jarrett, in his famous Cologne concert of 1975 (The Köln Concert), played freely in tonal styles in improvisations lasting 20 to 30 minutes, without ever becoming boring or leaving his audience behind. Now, two or three decades later, the shock has worn off, and free jazz, as it is known, has become one of a number of established ways of improvising, alongside bebop, New Orleans jazz and other styles.

All of these ideas in this chapter will help you develop your improvising skills. You need to work systematically at rhythm, pitch and harmony, as we've done in the previous chapters; but combining a rhythmic pattern, a snatch of melody or a particular chord or short sequence, discovered in your more detailed work, with some of the freer ideas we've looked at here, will build your confidence and lead to more inventive playing. Always strive to be as creative and imaginative as you can!

Chapter summary

○ *Doodle* at the keyboard; get a flow of ideas going and enjoy the sound of the piano.

○ Sometimes play with definite starting-points; at other times play as your mood dictates, until something more focused emerges.

○ Explore extremes of dynamics, texture and speed. Try different rhythmic styles and time signatures.

○ Explore the full range of piano sonorities. Try playing in two parts. Just enjoy the sound for its own sake.

○ Listen to a jazz recording and copy a particular feature or aspect you like.

Chapter 6   # Putting it all Together

> Suddenly, I discovered that my legs were in a condition of great excitement. They twitched as though charged with electricity and betrayed a considerable and rather dangerous desire to jerk me from my seat. The rhythm of the music, which had seemed so unnatural at first, was beginning to jerk me from my seat. It wasn't the feeling of ease in the joints of the feet and toes which might be caused by a Strauss waltz; no, much more energetic, material, independent, as though one encountered a balking horse, which is absolutely impossible to master.
>
> EDWARD A. BERLIN

In this chapter we look at ways to approach learning the head and solo section of any piece from the syllabus, and then take three particular pieces and demonstrate how the main ideas of Part I can be applied. In the process, and at the risk of repeating some of the material from earlier chapters, we will pull the various strands together, summarize the ground so far covered and put some of the theory into practice. For those taking the exams, the approaches used here will be particularly useful at Grades 1–3.

Learning the head

Learning a piece has several aspects to it. The first and most obvious is that you have to achieve technical control of the piece and be physically able to realize it. The second, particularly important in jazz, is that you achieve a clear and detailed aural image of the piece in your head, on which to base your improvising. This includes the feel, the groove, the melody, the length of the form, the chord sequence and any guideline figures or pitches given.

Get a sense of the whole thing

Rather than hammer in straightaway with the mechanics of learning the notes, the first task when learning a piece is to get a sense of its overall shape and general character. Listen to the Board's published CD for the grade, or another player's interpretation of the chosen piece, with the aim of getting an idea of the style. Or play the piece through very slowly as best you can, missing out the difficult bits but doing your best to get a sense of the whole—perhaps get someone more skilled to help you.

An important point is to try and build the musical character, dynamics, accents and phrasing into your learning process from the start. Learn the phrasing along with the notes straightaway, if necessary sacrificing pitch accuracy to begin with for a sense of the rhythmic character, shapes and gestures of the tune. The sense of the gesture and the rhythmic character is as important as the pitches and rhythms themselves, and can create a lively and stylish piece of music and a positive learning experience within five minutes of beginning work.

Focus on the detail

Once you have a sense of the overall shape, listen again to the piece and focus on more detailed elements to guide your learning.

Activities

1 *Title.* Look at the title. In jazz the titles of tunes are often colourful or tell you something about the character of the piece. Occasionally nothing is revealed, because the name relates to something personal to the composer or is simply a throw-away name, but sometimes the title can help you gain an understanding of what kind of playing or improvising is required. In the books of graded pieces we've also added a character word or phrase above the music to help guide your playing.

2 *Tempo.* How fast is the piece? Look at the metronome marking and set up a pulse at that tempo in your head. Perhaps click your fingers on beats 2 and 4.

3 *Feel.* Look at the feel indication. All jazz tunes will have a marking of some kind at the top to indicate whether they are in swing or straight 8s, and whether there is a particular rhythmic style or groove in mind. Do a bit of research to ensure you are using the intended feel, though the performances on the CDs by grade will illustrate what is required. It is *always* worth taking time to find recordings of pieces in the feel shown, to get a clear idea of the kind of sound the composer originally wanted. At the foot of each piece in the graded albums we've given some related listening, which you'll find a useful starting-point and aural guide.

4 *Dynamics.* Look for any dynamic markings. Is the piece generally at one level (loud or soft) or does it rise and fall, growing towards a climax at a certain point? In jazz often the dynamics are left more to the discretion of the performer, but the general character should be clear and there will be some dynamics given.

5 *Phrasing and texture.* Look to see whether the texture is generally smooth or is broken into shorter phrases, with various kinds of accents. What markings are there to give a sense of the character? Is the melody in the left or right hand? Is the left hand doing a bass-line, some choppy stabs or sustained chords? Are there any block chords across both hands?

6 *Routine.* Get a sense early on of the shape of the whole piece. Are any of the sections repeated, either by being written out in full or because repeat marks

are used? Identify the head and the solo section. Count through the solo bars and spot any sections that repeat. Work out what kinds of chord progressions are used. Are there any II–V–I progressions in the piece? Is it a twelve-bar blues? Is there a D.C. or D.S.? Where does the music go back to? Is there a Coda?

Learning the notes

Remember that the aim is to learn to play the given material accurately and with control and to know how the piece sounds in your head. Some musicians, when learning a tune, work more from the notation; others more by ear. The best ones are able to do both, and you should go through both sets of activities set out below to get the best from the material given.

Activities

Learning the piece by ear

1   Listen to the recording of the piece on the Board's CD or a tape of a friend playing the piece. Find the main tune or melody, perhaps omitting the introduction (if there is one) to begin with. Find the bit that repeats itself most often or the one that is easiest—you can fill in the harder bits later.

2   Hum or sing the opening phrases to yourself in small chunks, out loud along with the recording. Go as slowly as you like and repeat each section as many times as you need to—get it absolutely right. At this stage it doesn't matter if you can only manage a bar or a phrase at a time. Your memory will improve as you work more in this way.

   The most important thing is *not* to learn it wrong, because then you will have to unlearn it later. Don't go on until you've cracked it, and always listen to yourself carefully. Are you definitely singing the right pitches?

3   Once you can sing back a whole phrase, find the first note on the piano and work the melody out on the keyboard a note at a time, singing as you go. Then check it with the CD or tape. Move on, until you have a whole section of perhaps four or eight bars memorized.

4   Now turn to the left hand and do the same with the bass-line. Often this is more repetitive and should not take so long. Work on the obvious things first—a prominent rhythm, the very beginning, the very end—whatever is distinctive and most easily memorable.

5   Now look at the chord symbols. Play the chords one by one very slowly above the bass-line—do they fit?

6   Use the notated part to help you if you get stuck, perhaps to find the first note on the keyboard or to work out the difficult parts note by note. Use the score as a reference for the parts that you can't get clear by ear.

In the long run learning the piece by ear can lead to a much greater sense of security and knowledge of the piece than learning from notation.

Learning the piece from the notation

1   Start off simply by reading the piece through slowly, a section at a time. Work hands separately at first, avoiding the temptation to put both hands together before they are secure. If you put the hands together too soon, your image of the piece will have holes in it that will take longer to fill later, and you may find places where you feel unnecessary tension in performance because you are worrying about a more insecure passage.

2   Once you think you have it, listen to the recording on the Board's CD for points of style and accuracy.

Those with good notation skills will have to work by ear too to some extent, and those working by ear should work with the notation as far as they can. By the time you reach Grade 5, an ability both to pick up points of style from a heard piece and to play accurately and musically from given notation will be important for *all* candidates. Particularly towards Grades 4 and 5, working exclusively with notation or exclusively by ear are no longer viable options and a combination of the two is the only way to secure the flexible and relaxed control of both head and chord sequence required. The syllabus is designed to promote working using both these methods, and it is important to get into the habit of working by ear *and* with the notes as soon as you can.

Beware of moments of stress caused by troublesome corners, for example places with technical difficulties, or where you transfer from notated head to solo section, or vice versa. This can be done by making a distinction in your own mind between practising particular moments and practising the whole thing. Don't waste time by always starting at the beginning and playing right through to the end. Sometimes this is appropriate to get the flow going, and a play-through can certainly be helpful when preparing to improvise, because it gives you a chance to relax into the tune and build up some energy. But if there is a particular bar which is causing technical problems, work on that bar separately in a very focused way, note by note.

Iron out not only the technical problem but also any internal psychological tension or panic that may be associated with this bar. Aim for over-confident, and if necessary even bored security of control, so that you can save your nerves for taking real risks with the music in performance.

Learning the solo section

Often the chord sequence of the solo section is based on the chords of the head, so you may find you have in some ways learnt the sequence in learning the tune itself. However, it's worth taking time to learn the sequence thoroughly, so that your improvising is relaxed and confident.

In Chapter 3 we looked in detail at the nuts and bolts of learning a chord sequence, so only a summary is required here.

1   Count the length of the whole sequence, noting how long each chord lasts.

2 Learn the bass-line by singing and then playing it. Be confident about where the chords and bass-line change.

3 Build up the chords from the bass-line, adding the 3rds and 5ths to make triads, and then adding the 7ths. Play through the sequence using two- and three-note voicings. Do this in both hands, as you may wish to use the chord shapes in your right hand too.

4 Find the guide tones (the 3rds and 7ths) and trace them through the sequence.

5 Notice the movement of the inner lines created by the movement of these guide tones. Play the inner lines in simple form and then embellish them melodically and rhythmically.

6 Play up and down the chord tones, focusing on each degree in turn.

7 Begin to invent phrases which use the chord tones to embellish the inner lines, using passing notes of various kinds.

You'll also find that working in turn on the cadences and other important progressions which recur several times will help get the structure in your head.

As you learn different tunes, you'll discover patterns and chord sequences which recur, particularly of course between different blues tunes, and you'll find learning the sequence gets easier, as you can refer back to these other tunes. In a moment we'll look at improvising on the two Grade 1 tunes, 'Bags' Groove' and 'Prove you Groove', but compare first their chord charts:

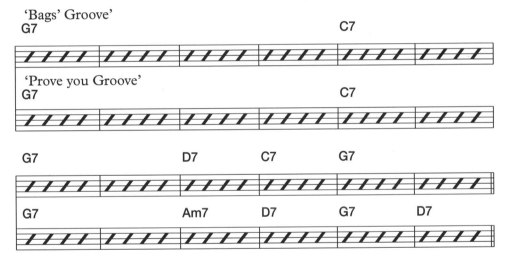

You'll notice that it's only at the end that the chords are different, 'Bags' Groove' ending with a V–IV–I movement and 'Prove you Groove' with a II–V–I (and then a chord V by way of return). So if you've already learnt 'Bags' Groove', it is these final bars which should be the focus of your practice when working on 'Prove you Groove'. Much of the character difference between the two tunes will come from the rhythmic character, defined by the feel indication and the tempo.

Practising the improvisation

Once you know the notes and have learnt the sequence, the fun begins! Now you can play around with the tune, using all the techniques and approaches we've looked at, to make the piece your own. Let's look in detail at three of the Grade 1 pieces, 'Bags' Groove', 'Prove you Groove' and 'Perdido', beginning with 'Bags' Groove'.

right hand

Activities

1 Look at the guideline pitches given for the solo section for 'Bags' Groove'. Each of the three boxes gives a selection of notes from the ♭3 pentatonic scale on G, firstly two sets of three pitches either side of the key note, and then the whole scale in third inversion. Practise this scale to help make your solos more fluent, perhaps by playing the scale (say, in third inversion) against the left hand given:

2 Try different inversions of the scale. How do these affect the sound of your melody? Was one easier than another? As you get more confident, practise moving smoothly from one inversion to another, as the guideline pitches indicate, to give yourself more scope. Also try playing the same notes up and down the octave later in the improvisation to add a new colour to the sound.

3 Generally speaking, avoid the trap of always playing the notes in the same order as they're given in the note box, with just a syncopation or two thrown in. Perhaps start with the outside two and work in:

or go from top to bottom:

or focus on one or two of the pitches suggested, and construct an improvisation upon them.

4 Let's work a little more at the notes of this scale and build improvisations on different degrees of it. First try basing one on the root:

then the 3rd:

and finally the 5th:

5   Try varying stepwise movement:

with movement up and down triad shapes or jumping across a wider range:

6   Find other scales which would work well over this sequence. Mixolydian on G would work well over the G7 chords, but watch out for the B natural which would clash with the B♭ of the C7 chord in bar 5.

left hand

The melodies we've created here will all work with the left-hand guideline pitches exactly as they're given (which, as you've probably noticed, are the guide tones for this sequence). But there are many ways to enliven a sequence of semibreves such as this, and let's now explore some of those ways by looking at the solo section for 'Prove you Groove'.

Activities

Let's try some rhythm exercises in the left hand.

1   Play the left hand as written or even simply the bass-line in steady semibreves:

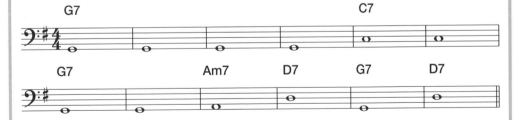

2   Now play the bass-line in crotchets on beat 1, like this:

3   Then on beat 2, like this:

4   Also play through the bass-line on beats 3 and 4 and on the upbeat quavers too.

5   Be strict to begin with, but once you get going relax and try varying this more. Perhaps start with a variation where you play on the first beat in the first bar, the second beat in the second bar and then more variations thereafter:

6   Add in an offbeat quaver or two:

7   Try an upbeat embellishment into the first note of each bar:

And so on.

8   Finally, the notes section to this piece gives ideas about reusing the vamp from the head of the piece in the solo section as well. Think of the notes you could play in bars 21–2 to follow this pattern and construct a strong left hand for the whole of the solo section.

 9   Listen to track 41 to hear some of these ideas demonstrated.

hands together

Many of these ideas can also be used to loosen up the right hand. Keep the left hand playing semibreves as given in the music and work through the following activities.

Activities

1   Choose one of the right-hand pitches given in the first box (say, the G), and displace it through the bar like this:

2   Now take a short rhythm and do the same:

etc.

3   Now create a short improvisation using only the note G, with rhythms like this as a basis:

etc.

If you have trouble keeping in time, use a metronome or some kind of regular click from a computer to keep you steady. Set it to regular crotchets at first, but then try setting it to click on beats 2 and 4 to emphasize the backbeat.

How many different rhythmic options are there? How distinctive can you make your solo by using space, dynamics, phrasing or touch?

Now let's move on to some question and answer exercises.

4   First set up a simple two-bar repeated question over the given left-hand part, using a motive of your choice, perhaps something like this:

Notice that bars 3–4, 7–8 and 11–12 are left empty at this stage. Be sure to count these gaps accurately!

5 Now try filling each gap with a two-bar improvisation of your own, for example:

6 Now try the same exercise, but this time give yourself an answer to work with in bars 3–4, 7–8 and 11–12 and fill the gaps with questions.

Remember to vary the improvisations each time, by choosing different rhythms, varying the pitches or dynamics or by leaving spaces at different points in the two-bar gap. Vary levels of intensity too, sometimes playing virtually nothing at all and simply counting in your head, while at other times playing on every beat. Don't be afraid, if the spirit moves you, to ignore the guideline pitches altogether—as we've done above—as long as you move back to them later so that your playing retains a structure of some sort.

To begin with, it's important to keep the left-hand accompaniment as simple and rhythmically clear as you can, so that you have enough technical flexibility to create an interesting melody. However, even those Grade 1 pieces which have only semibreves notated in the left hand can often be varied with a few syncopations or with one of the simple vamps and bass-lines given at the end of this book.

At the start, gain confidence in the right hand and left hand independently. If possible, find a second player to put in the left hand for you so that you can concentrate exclusively on the right, or tape yourself playing one of the hands.

When you come to put both hands together, there are some step-by-step exercises you can do to develop your confidence and skills. Let's demonstrate these by looking at the solo section for 'Perdido'.

1   Start simply by playing the left hand in semibreves as given, concentrating on counting the sequence accurately and knowing when to change chord.

2   Now try a simple question and answer between left and right hand, perhaps based on a simple rhythmic motive in the left hand, like this:

3   Now try the other way round. Lead with a right-hand melody and let the left hand comment and respond:

4   Finally place left-hand kicks so that they reinforce the rhythm of the right-hand tune:

There are some more ideas about putting right and left hands together in Chapter 2.

On the CD which accompanies Grade 1 there are performances of all three of these tunes to give you something to aim for. Listen also to the various pieces recorded to get an idea of the kinds of embellishment you could do on the repeat of the head. Remember though that your own version should *not* sound identical to these; there may be ideas you particularly like and want to copy, but make up your own version, following the tempo, groove and chord sequence given.

There are plenty of ideas here for developing your improvisations. Begin with short improvisations, once through the solo section, but as you get more confident, move on to longer solos, playing through a chorus several times. Get a flow going and keep going round and round, pushing yourself to explore different ideas each time, and building up the energy level as the solo progresses. Get to know the tunes inside out. Play them from memory. In performance, be as inventive as you can, but beware of repeating yourself or of going on too long (in the exam, remember to improvise for the number of bars indicated). Given the choice, always leave them wanting more!

Chapter summary

○ When learning a piece, aim for full technical control and also a clear and detailed aural image of the piece in your head.

○ Get a sense of the overall shape and style of a piece first; concentrate on its musical character—its dynamics, accents, phrasing, feel and groove. Aim to capture the character in the notes straightaway.

○ If you learn from notation, try also to learn part of the piece by ear: listen to it on the Board's CD and try to grasp some aspect of it—rhythm, part of the melody, the ending—by ear. Conversely, for those working mainly by ear, try to use the notation at least in part. Whichever method you use, work very slowly, aiming to get whole sections absolutely right, rather than skimming through the whole thing.

○ Learn the form of the solo section thoroughly: count the bars and the length of each chord, sing and play the bass-line, build up triads and 7ths from the bass-line, find the guide tones and inner lines.

○ Look at the guideline right-hand pitches in the solo and play the scale from which they're taken; consider other scales which you might use. Build melodic phrases from the various notes of these scales.

○ Practise the left hand in the solo, playing the bass-line in different rhythms and voicing the chords in different ways.

○ Put your improvisation together, slowly at first! Use question and answer techniques or lead with one hand and respond with the other. Keep the left hand simple, perhaps using left-hand kicks to reinforce the right-hand tune. Keep any performance short, to the point and as distinctive as you can make it within the style.

Part II
MOVING ON

For me, that's where the music always has to be—
on the edge — in between the known and the
unknown, and you have to keep pushing it towards
the unknown otherwise you and it die.

STEVE LACY

Chapter 7   # Rhythm Skills

> I mean, a Sousa march should groove. Viennese waltzes
> groove. Someone playing . . . a Bach solo violin sonata should
> be grooving . . . You should feel . . . from phrase to phrase and
> within phrases . . . a forward rhythmic flow.
>
> JEROME HARRIS

We began our rhythm work in Part I by looking at some basic principles: pulse, subdivisions, the backbeat, the three most common grooves, rhythmic placement, rhythmic flexibility and basic improvisation using question and answer and echo techniques. In this more advanced chapter we'll work through these principles more thoroughly, using more demanding exercises.

We'll explore rhythmic placement in more depth, looking in detail at the various possibilities within 4/4. We'll build on this rhythm work with short improvisations using scale shapes and simple melodies, and learn how to extend solos by developing a musical idea or motive. We'll look at how to create effective accompaniments to your melody work ('comping'), and we'll end by looking afresh at common jazz grooves and how to put these across as a pianist. Throughout, our aims remain to encourage creative possibilities by achieving rhythmic *flexibility* and *control*.

Semiquavers

In Part I your rhythm work was mostly based on crotchets, quavers and minims, occasionally with their dotted values. From Grade 4 onwards you will find semiquavers appearing in the pieces more often, and you are likely to want to start using semiquavers in your improvising. Begin to add these to your regular rhythm practice when you feel ready, slotting them into the placement and question and answer exercises in Part I.

When vocalizing semiquavers, the syllables 'one - er - an - er' are easy to say repeatedly and fit well with the ones we used earlier. They make rhythms that sound like this when you say them:

1		an	er	**2**		an	er	**3**		an	er	**4**		an	er
1	er	an		**2**	er	an		**3**	er	an		**4**	er	an	
1	er		er	**2**	er		er	**3**	er		er	**4**	er		er

Notice that the 'an' on the third semiquaver stays in the same place as a reference point within the beat in both quaver and semiquaver rhythms.

Syncopation and anticipation

A cornerstone of jazz rhythm is *syncopation*, which means stressing notes other than the main beats of the bar. Often this takes the form of *anticipation*, or playing a note early. This creates surprise, adds rhythmic tension and is a way of varying a phrase over a fixed pulse. Even the simple anticipation of a single note, played a quaver early, can transform a phrase, as this:

can become this:

or this:

If you are coming to this book as a classical musician, you will be used to the importance and strength of the first and third beats of a bar of 4/4. This is, if you like, the groove of classical music. The beats before those, such as beat 4 in 4/4, sound *un*stressed and lead up to the strong beats (an effect called *anacrusis*; plural, 'anacruses'). You'll find examples of straightforward anacruses in the jazz pieces for Grades 4 and 5, for example, the opening of 'In a different light'.

But jazz often puts more stress on beats 2 and 4 (the backbeat in swing and rock grooves), and it often anticipates beats 1 and 3, by a quaver. These anticipations are themselves stressed, for example:

Also, sometimes notes that may *appear* to be anacruses include anticipated main beats which need to be stressed, creating a different pattern:

These are not upbeats; they are actually first beats that have been displaced to become anticipations. As you work at the materials for Grades 4 and 5, be sensitive to these rhythmic stresses and patterns, and develop your feel for jazz phrasing. Notice too how this more asymmetrical phrasing creates spaces in the phrase, which are emphasized by the use of long or short notes.

Polyrhythms

These different patterns can build up into *polyrhythms*, when one rhythm or pulse is superimposed over another. If the stress is moved around in a regular way you can create exciting interactions, such as:

In this case the right hand is effectively moving in 3 over a steady 4/4 pulse. A single rich and complex effect is made from two simple rhythms. Here are some more examples of the same kinds of effect:

Rhythmic placement

In Chapter 1 we began our study of this by placing individual notes and short phrases on each crotchet and quaver in turn. This helped to develop flexibility in deciding where in the bar to begin or end a phrase, and how much space to leave from one phrase to another. In this section we're going to develop this placement idea more methodically, and we'll explore ways in which you can use it in your improvising.

Single notes

When all's said and done, there are only eight quavers in a 4/4 bar! So if we're playing only one note in the bar, there are obviously four places in the bar to play a note *on* the beat, and another four where we can play it *off* the beat—eight in all.

┌─ Activities ─────────────────────────────────

1   As a revision of the work from Chapter 1, begin by clapping these rhythms:

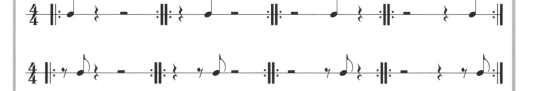

2   Now repeat, this time playing a single note or chord on the piano, like this:

3   Try these exercises, and all those given below, both straight and swing, and in a range of tempos and dynamics. All the exercises are given in 4/4, which is the easiest and also most common place to start in the style, but you should also try them in time signatures like 3/4 and even 5/4.

Phrases

In practice, of course, we tend to play in phrases rather than always in single notes. So let's explore the same idea, this time using a two-note phrase instead of one note. This will cover all the possible combinations of two crotchet beats in a 4/4 bar.

Activities

1   Here are the various ways two notes may be placed in a bar, this time with a bar's gap and with the pattern moving in two-bar cycles. Clap and play these different patterns.

43

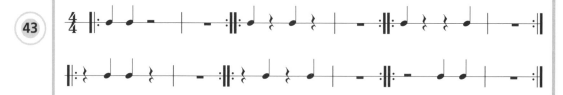

2   Repeat the exercise, this time using the *offbeats*:

44

3 When you're ready, move on to three and four notes in the bar, again in two-bar phrases. First, on the beat:

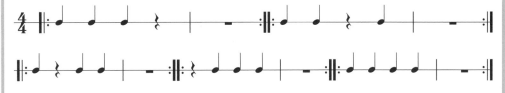

4 and then off the beat:

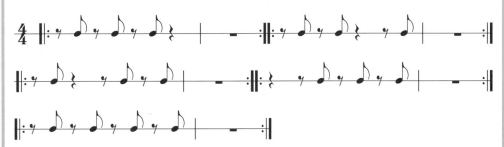

5 Now extend these activities by:
   (*a*) improvising one-bar answers in the gap;
   (*b*) moving the rhythms to bar 2, leaving bar 1 as a space; then improvise in bar 1;
   (*c*) playing each rhythmic pattern through a chord sequence, comping in the left hand using the repeated rhythm shown.

The chart below summarizes these rhythmic possibilities—keep it handy for the further practice routines that follow. From this chart we can derive almost all the simple basic rhythms of jazz. If you can clap these rhythms in any combination, on any beat or half-beat, then say them and play them through with one note on a piano, you are well on your way to becoming a jazz musician!

Placement Combinations in 4/4

on the beat

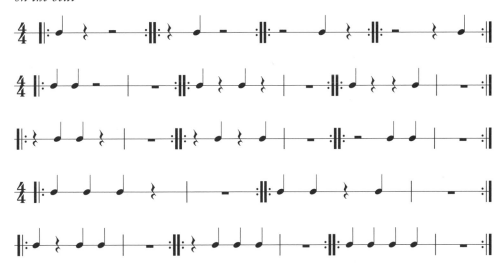

off the beat

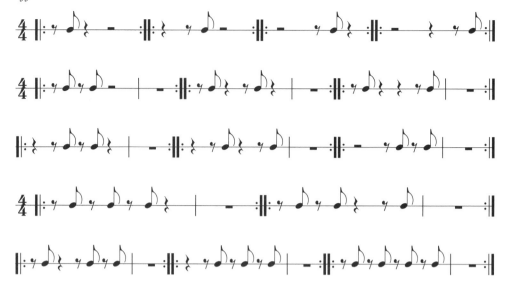

Now let's apply these ideas to your playing in different ways. Remember that jazz is a rhythmic music above all. So it is vital that whatever notes we play, we are rhythmically positive and accurate.

Scale and melody practice

Chapter 16 gives a range of ideas to explore when practising scales. Here we look at ways to develop your work on rhythm by using scales and scale shapes. What follows is only a selection of possible exercises you can use. As you play through tunes or discover problems in your practice, adapt and alter the ideas, or make up your own.

Regular rhythms

⌐ **Activities** ──────────────

1   We'll begin with simple regular rhythms, doing basic counting exercises as well as scales. Beginning at a tempo of about crotchet = 70, practise a scale of Dorian on D, firstly in crotchets and then in quavers.

2   When you are ready, try triplet quavers.

3   Now experiment with where you put the stress. Try stressing the first beat of the bar, or the second and fourth beats, like a rock beat:

4   Now stress all the offbeat quavers, in both swing and straight feels:

5   Try moving from crotchets to quavers every bar, then every half-bar and finally every beat:

6   Start very slowly and get steadily faster, or the other way round.

7   Move from straight to swung groove on the barline.

8   Simulate a swing groove by setting the metronome to click on beats 2 and 4 of a 4/4 bar and playing a scale in quavers.

Adding space

Now let's add space to this rhythm practice. This will help develop flexibility by using less predictable rhythmic patterns. Remember, don't allow your critical faculties to switch off. Listen carefully to yourself all the time, and work using your internal clock and with a metronome or click.

Activities

1   Choose four notes from a scale. For example, let's take the first four notes of C major: C, D, E and F. First, play the four notes as an ascending pattern, like this:

2   Now play them in a rhythmic pattern that introduces a space. Perhaps this:

or this:

Keep the pattern going, leaving out different notes in turn:

3 Now try the scale again, this time descending, over a longer pattern of quavers.

Remember: concentrate on keeping the pulse going accurately and positively throughout.

4 Use rhythms from the placement chart, with the spaces they contain, to play your scales. Try it with and without a metronome:

or for more advanced players:

Improvise in the space

Scales are useful in themselves, but we rarely want to play just straight scales when we improvise. You need to be able to lead from other ideas into and away from scales. Working on fingering is an important part of developing this skill: make sure you know several fingerings for each scale you play. Let's now combine our scale and rhythmic practice with some real improvising, using the placement chart as a basis.

Activities

1 Take a simple crotchet rhythm from the placement chart and use it to play part of a scale, leaving a one-bar gap:

2 Repeat the exercise several times, filling the gap with your own improvisation. Start by using the same notes:

3   Once you've had a couple of goes at this, try to continue the phrase begun by the scale:

4   Then try to lead back into the scale from your improvised phrase:

Using these ideas we find we can develop our grasp of jazz rhythms by playing simple scale shapes in rhythms taken from the placement chart. We can extend this further by adding space and then improvising in the space. Let's now broaden these skills by looking at other ways to develop rhythm.

Developing your improvisation

A common problem faced by inexperienced players is how to keep a solo going—we seem to run out of steam after only four or eight bars. It seems incredible that jazz players can produce a flow of fresh-sounding music that continues for several minutes.

The answer is, of course, that they are not inventing new ideas bar by bar. Instead they are taking a single idea or motive and finding interesting ways to develop it or use it again in a different way. They are trying to exhaust the possibilities of one idea before moving onto another.

A *motive* is simply a short musical idea, for example a fragment of melody or a simple rhythm. Jazz musicians think of all kinds of ingenious ways to build long phrases and different shapes from short motives. For a good example listen to Miles Davis' interpretation of 'Bye Bye Blackbird' on his album *Round Midnight*. In Chapter 8 we'll look at developing melodic motives, but for now we will work with rhythmic ideas.

Repetition and simple embellishment

Activities

Here is an example of a short, two-note rhythmic motive:

1   The most obvious and often under-used way of developing a motive is simply to repeat it. Don't be afraid to emphasize a good phrase by baldly repeating it, either straight:

2   or at a different place in the bar, sometimes on the beat, sometimes off. You can use the rhythmic placement chart for ideas:

By itself this can set up a tension, a need to change the following time, or to go from the repeated phrase into something else. Now invent your own two-note phrase and do the same.

3   You can take the phrase and play it backwards (*inversion*):

4   You can rhythmically *embellish* your idea, for example by leading into it:

5   or leading out from it:

6   or perhaps by adding different embellishments each time:

Subdivision

Another form of rhythmic embellishment involves subdividing beats.

Activities

1   Clap this basic phrase:

2   Vary it by turning the first beat into triplets:

3 Move the triplet through the bar beat by beat, keeping the overall rhythmic shape of the phrase intact, like this:

4 Intensify the phrase by adding another triplet:

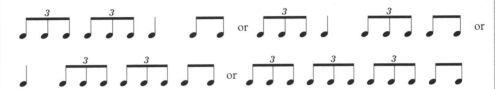

5 Omit a note:

In this way a single motive can inspire a whole range of possible variations.

6 It's also possible to lengthen or shorten part of a phrase by doubling or halving the values of each note. In this next example notice how the note values of the motive in the first bar are halved in the second (*diminution*) and lengthened in the third (*augmentation*):

Finally, don't forget that in swing time you can use all three notes of the triplet, not just two as before:

With practice you can also use semiquavers:

7 Now invent your own motive and try out each of the techniques described.

Developing rhythmic or melodic motives like this is one of the commonest ways to create a sense of order and structure in an improvisation or a composition. 'Worrying' a motive, exploring the limits of its creative possibilities, is an enjoyable part of improvising in any style.

Find one-bar rhythmic motives from the pieces you are learning and use them regularly as material to work through the exercises in this chapter and those in Chapter 1. Take only one or, at the most, two contrasting rhythms and really internalize them over a long period. Practise them every day for several weeks and use them in as many ways as you can. By getting even a small number of these rhythms under your belt and varying them, you will have a wide enough range of rhythmic vocabulary on which to base your solos by Grade 5.

To summarize these rhythm exercises and to give you a checklist to work through, try each of the following with your chosen one-bar rhythms:

1 place the rhythm on each quaver in the bar in turn
2 play it in straight and swing phrasing
3 play it at a range of tempos
4 anticipate by a quaver notes that are on the beat
5 use the rhythm in your scale practice
6 use the rhythm as a vamp to play through a chord sequence
7 embellish it with extra material
8 vary it with augmentation and diminution
9 play the rhythm in the left hand while improvising in the right, or vice versa.

Rhythm and comping

An important area of work for the jazz pianist is comping (short for 'accompaniment'). Comping involves creating a rhythmic and harmonic background for your own melodies or for other players' solos. The technique is based mostly on chords and simple rhythmic figurations, usually in the left hand.

We will look in the next chapter at the chord progressions you might use in comping. For now, we'll concentrate on the rhythmic side, and look at how to use the principles you have learned so far to create simple and effective accompaniments. In general, being rhythmically interesting is more important than being harmonically complex.

In Part I you will have practised introducing simple offbeat chords at various points in the bar with your left hand while you played solos with the right. The next stage is to develop *co-ordination* between the two hands.

Developing co-ordination

Activities

1 Start with the following basic patterns. Beginning with several bars of each, work towards changing the pulses between the hands every half-bar.

2 Now begin to introduce rhythmic motives. Keep the pulse going in one hand while in the right hand play a chosen rhythmic motive, perhaps a rhythm from a piece you are learning. Now swap hands.

3 Tapping a regular rhythm with one hand, try some simple rhythmic improvising with the other. Again, swap hands.

4 Go through these exercises in straight and swing feels in 4/4, then in 3/4.

5 To get the rhythm in your whole body, you could extend these exercises by tapping your feet as well, nodding your head, or swaying from side to side. Try all the possibilities: left hand with right foot and vice versa, nodding your head while you tap with your right hand, and so on.

Now let's move to the piano.

Activities

1 On C7, try playing steady crotchets in the left hand and a quaver scale in the right:

2 Now swap hands:

3 Work through the patterns of alternating hands that you tapped out above.

4 Change the chord in the second bar of the two-bar sequence to F7:

5 Now develop it into a II–V–I sequence, like this:

6 Next, try playing a walking bass in steady crotchets with the left hand, with a different pattern in the right:

7 Play a scale in the right hand with a simple vamp in the left:

8 Finally, take a piece from your own repertoire and work through the chord sequence in the same way. Use rhythms from the chart in the Appendix and develop a feel for playing a range of different repeated patterns.

Adding improvisation

Let's explore how these comping ideas can work in playing a piece of your own, using as an example the familiar twelve-bar blues sequence in G. We'll begin by playing steady chords in the left hand and improvising with just a few notes in the right, say the first part of a Mixolydian on G scale:

Activities

1 Start by developing the left hand. Turn the chords into a vamp, such as this one, singing or clapping the rhythm first to get it into your head:

2   Now invent a right-hand part. Start by using only a couple of notes, say G and B♭. Don't worry if it sounds a little stilted at first: your aim is to keep the left-hand pattern steady—the right hand can take care of itself!

3   Now vary the left-hand pattern, perhaps using one of these:

4   Once you feel at home with a few comp patterns, allow your right-hand improvisation to influence what your left hand plays. For example:

or combine several rhythms that you have learned separately.

5   You can invent more 'pushing' exercises of your own, where the left-hand rhythm follows the right hand. The right-hand tune here, for instance, seems naturally to demand its left-hand accompaniment:

Eventually, you will be able to lead with the solo in the right hand and the left will follow.

6   Be systematic as you practise left-hand vamps. Aim to be able to play the rhythms starting at any point in the bar, on or off the beat, in straight or swing feels. For example, if you start with this:

Try placing it on every quaver beat of the bar:

Choose rhythms that fit the style of the pieces you're playing.

7   As you learn new chord sequences, use them to play the vamps that you know. For example, here is the vamp we played through earlier, but now using the chords of the middle 8 from Charlie Shavers' 'Undecided':

You'll find that as you practise you develop more rhythmic flexibility, but you must make sure that you first learn the patterns properly.

Common grooves

Let's now look at the sound and notation of some of the most common grooves used by jazz musicians, which you will come across in the syllabus. Most of them are easy to recognize when played by an ensemble, and so we've given some examples on the CD accompanying this book. In each case:

1 Clap along with the given rhythms;
2 Sing and then play the melodies and bass-lines;
3 Focus on the way the beat is subdivided and how the melodies are phrased in the various styles;
4 Listen to the classic tracks suggested.

Swing

'It don't mean a thing if it ain't got that swing': the title of Duke Ellington's piece says it all! A feel for swing is essential for playing what is called 'straight ahead' jazz—the standard repertoire from the 1930s to the 1950s. This music demands a relaxed but positive driving pulse (felt broadly in 12/8 but written in 4/4); rhythmic flexibility over that pulse (pushing forwards or backwards around the solid beat, anticipating and syncopating); and internal dynamics and phrasing appropriate to the style, usually over a crotchet walking-bass line. Swing is an important feature of modern jazz too, and you'll hear it in new pieces, along with other grooves.

Listen carefully to track 45 on the CD. Two grooves, one swing and one straight, alternate in four-bar sections. Listen to how, though the *speed* remains constant, the subdivisions and stresses make the rhythm *feel* different.

Led from the ride cymbal in a band context, swing grooves often seem slower or more spacious, even though they may be going at the same speed as other straight feels. Sometimes a swing groove feels relaxed or laid back—perhaps the players are actually playing fractionally behind the beat, or at least they make it feel that way. At other times it feels on the front of the beat, pushing on, driving forward.

At the bottom of the texture the bass-line contains full fat crotchets that fill the whole space of each beat. The ride is dancing away at the top, filling the space with its rich sound, always walking forward. Sometimes there will be a lot of space in the texture, sometimes the texture will be complex and full of layers, each with their own strong and weak beats. Because the ride cymbal is at the top of the rhythmic texture, swing often seems to float, very bright and airy in sound quality. Whatever line the ride cymbal plays, it will always give some sense of the backbeat in its emphasis on beats 2 and 4.

Listen closely to the drumming of Art Blakey on his Jazz Messengers albums for really solid and exciting swing playing. Almost any recorded jazz pianist will play in swing, but listen especially to Oscar Peterson's *Travellin' On* for an accessible introduction to this style of playing.

2 feel and 4 feel

There are a number of commonly used ways of varying intensity within a swing groove to create or release tension. Changing from a 2 feel to a 4 feel at the same speed and within the same pulse is one of these.

46 Track 46 has the opening 16 bars of 'I'm beginning to see the Light' played by a trio, the first 8 bars in a 2 feel, the second in a 4 feel. Notice how the second 8 bars *feel* more energetic and move forward with more drive, because the bass-line is moving mainly in crotchets. Notice too that thinking in a 2 feel does not preclude the bass player from putting in the odd crotchet here and there for variety. The underlying ten-to-ten on the drums remains constant, though the drummer may choose to leave out more and *imply* the ten-to-ten rhythm more in a 2 feel.

Rock

Although rock music is not strictly the domain of the syllabus, jazz musicians became attracted to the straight feel, rhythmic intensity and electric sounds of rock music virtually from its beginnings, and jazz began to interact with rock music a great deal in the 1960s and 1970s. Miles Davis led the way with his albums *In a Silent Way* and *Bitches Brew* and Weather Report's *Heavy Weather*, containing the well-known track 'Birdland', is another example of this style of jazz, sometimes called 'jazz-rock'. Look out also for the work of pianist Ramsey Lewis (particularly the track 'The In Crowd'), whose accessible style blends the rhythmic language of R'n'B, blues and rock. Chick Corea's Electric Band albums and the 1970s work of Herbie Hancock (especially albums like *Headhunters*), are other good places to start for keyboard players interested in the use of synthesizers and computers in the creation of complex electronic textures.

Rock grooves of all kinds are usually led from the bass-drum, which creates the characteristic sound of rock, along with the bass-line, often played by the electric bass. There are broadly two kinds of rock groove to consider up to Grade 5. The first is the conventional 8-beat rock, with the quavers played on the hi-hat:

Listen to this pattern played in the Billy Taylor tune 'I wish I knew' on track 47.

The second is the 16-beat rock, based on semiquavers, sometimes known as 'funk':

 Listen for this on track 48 ('Chameleon' by Herbie Hancock).

Notice how in both the bass-drum and snare are locked in a perpetual question and answer. Unlike swing, it is the snare that emphasizes the backbeat, and the bass-drum kicks along with the bass. In most pop music since the 1950s rock grooves tend to be more fixed, and the vocals take centre-stage in providing melodic and textural colour. In jazz, musicians tend to vary rock and funk grooves more, sometimes remaining completely fixed, but at others introducing all kinds of syncopations and anticipations, known as 'kicks', to vary the rhythm and manipulate the musical material as they play long solos.

The other main characteristic of rock grooves is their use of repeated bass-lines and melodic features, called *riffs*. *In a Silent Way* and *Headhunters* both use riffs to good effect.

Latin

Latin grooves also started to mix with jazz in the 1940s, and are another good example of the interaction of jazz with other popular styles. The music of Latin America is a separate and huge topic, with complex interactions and fusions across cultures. But because of the proximity of this region to North America and in particular the birthplace of jazz, New Orleans, the influence on jazz of latin music has never been far away.

Latin grooves are in straight feel and do not have a backbeat as such, but instead rely for their rhythmic character on another set of stresses across a 4/4 bar known as the clave (pronounced 'clah-vay'). There are many types of clave, but the most common, known as the 3 + 2 clave, goes like this:

 Track 49 plays this clave, alone and with Terry Seabrook's tune 'Mambo Country' (Grade 5).

The clave is also sometimes found with bars 1 and 2 transposed, as its reverse, the 2 + 3 clave. 'The Peanut Vendor' is a tune that features a 2 + 3 clave, including a riff that fits the melody like this:

Clap and play the two claves until you know them well.

Sometimes these rhythms are played by one percussionist as written above. But in a big salsa band the *whole* band sound, including bass-, kit or hand-held drums and percussion, and any other instruments including brass and voices, is seen as an expression of the particular clave, and sometimes no one instrument is actually playing the whole rhythm. Tito Puente's albums are good examples of the clave style, with some excellent piano playing and a variety of full band textures and improvising.

The two most familiar latin grooves to have found their way into jazz are the *bossa nova* and the *samba*.

Bossa nova

The bossa nova style became popular in the 1960s, particularly with tunes by Antonio Carlos Jobim such as 'The Girl from Ipanema'. The style is slow and often lyrical, and the clave is changed slightly to become:

On the piano you might play it like this:

Notice that the bass-line expresses the two-feel pulse, while the right hand plays the two-bar bossa nova rhythm.

There are many styles of bossa nova, both fast and slow. Some are closer to Latin American folk music, some come from jazz versions of the groove. Characteristics of bossa nova comping are the use of rich voicings and inner lines moving in counter-melodies under the main tune.

Samba

Samba began as the music of the Rio carnival. It is music for dancing to, or for moving down a carnival street, either at a stroll or a frenetic trot. It is usually in a fast 2 feel.

Listen to the tune 'One Note Samba' played on track 51. Let your body sway from left to right and think 'er-one, er-two, er-one, er-two' as you focus on the bass-drum. Notice how there is a slight accent on the second minim of each bar, more like 'er-one, er-TWO, er-one, er-TWO'.

In the carnival the 'two' is accented by an enormous drum called a 'surdo'. It leads the whole samba, while bells pick out a pattern based on quavers. In jazz sambas, the role of the surdo is taken by the bass-drum and the hi-hat or cymbals take the bell pattern. It fits together like this:

Notice how the final quaver of each bar has a particular stress and position in this rolling groove.

A pianist might play something simpler for a samba, for example, a bass-line in two with longer chords, like this:

Listen again to track 51 and hear how the pianist keeps the momentum of the samba going using fewer notes.

There are many other styles that are related to the samba, including Caribbean grooves like the calypso.

Notation

As in much jazz, the notation of latin grooves is not always consistent. Sometimes they will be written in 2/2, sometimes in 4/4. The clave often has a strong 2 feel, particularly in faster numbers, even though they may be written in four. On the other hand, in slower pieces in 2/2, there can often be a noticeable crotchet pulse. As always, the notation is only a general guide. You have to listen carefully to the music itself.

Jazz waltz

The jazz waltz is the most common 3/4 groove in jazz. In swing feel, the ride pattern of ten-to-ten changes to:

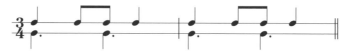

often with the characteristic offbeat stress on the 'and' of 2. On the piano this is often realized as:

For examples of jazz waltz, listen to Bill Evans' interpretations of 'Someday my prince will come' or 'Alice in Wonderland', both from the 1950s. There are also examples of jazz waltzes in the Board's books of jazz pieces, including Evans' '34Skidoo' (Grade 5).

Straight 8s

This sound is a relatively recent phenomenon, often used in European contemporary jazz. As straight feel jazz has developed, some players have wished to dispense altogether with the need for a backbeat, which can be seen as too rhythmically limiting or repetitive for some kinds of improvisation. Straight 8s is almost its own groove now, characterized by equal stress on all 4 beats, with the option of using latin or rock accents and inflections within the pulse. John Taylor, of the trio Azimuth, is one of a number of recent pianists to play straight 8s. The track 'Azimuth' is particularly worth listening to, as is Keith Jarrett's 'Your Song'.

Other grooves and time signatures

Most jazz is in 4/4, either straight or swung, and developing your rhythmic skills, placement and co-ordination in 4/4 is by far the most important skill in the early stages. But jazz has always grown and changed, and mingled with other music. In the 1960s it fused with rock and Latin American musics, and there have been similar dalliances with Indian music and South African jazz at various times. In the 1990s, British jazz has appropriated music as far ranging as Irish folk music and even classical music as a source of inspiration for improvising.

Because of this need to interact and grow, jazz has never confined itself exclusively to 4/4 time. Since the 1950s all kinds of time signatures have been used, including 3/4 and 5/4. Now you can find jazz in all kinds of duple, triple, and quadruple times, both simple and compound, and also asymmetric times, often still retaining elements of swing, latin or rock grooves and backbeats.

Some composers have experimented successfully with five-beat bars, often subdividing the beats into 3 + 2 or 2 + 3. The most famous example of this is Dave Brubeck's 'Take Five'. The Mahavishnu Orchestra has experimented with time signatures using other prime numbers (7, 11, 13, and so on), especially on their album *Birds of Fire*.

Chapter summary

○ *Syncopate* and *anticipate*, and develop your feel for jazz phrasing.

○ Add *semiquavers* to your rhythmic vocabulary.

○ Place chords and short phrases on all the beats and offbeats of a bar. Develop this using scale shapes and short improvisations.

○ Use *polyrhythm*.

○ Develop ways to keep an improvisation going, by trying out ways of transforming a rhythmic *motive*. Use the techniques of *embellishment, sub-division, augmentation* and *diminution*.

○ Create backgrounds for solos and melodies by *comping*. Develop co-ordination between the hands.

○ Listen to, identify, recreate and use the most familiar grooves: *swing, rock* and *jazz-rock*, the *clave* of *latin* rhythms, especially the *bossa nova* and the *samba, straight 8s*.

○ Explore the *jazz waltz* groove, and try patterns in 5/4 too.

Chapter 8   # Melody and Harmony

There are only two types of music—good and bad.

DUKE ELLINGTON

In this chapter we will add to your stock of useful melodic and harmonic ingredients. The more common of these can be used in improvisations across a wide range of jazz styles, for many types of tune. By familiarizing yourself with these basic materials, you will be in a position to work through the following chapters, each dealing with a specific jazz style.

We will go through some of the most common principles of jazz melody and harmony, all the time encouraging you to listen carefully to each element as it is introduced. Since good improvisation is based on an ability to hear clearly what is going on, the emphasis will be on listening to the qualities of intervals and chords, and applying these techniques to the pieces you are learning.

In melody we will look at the role intervals play in shaping a tune, and examine how different intervals can create consonance or dissonance, both within a tune and against the underlying harmony. We'll also add different notes to the triad tones and look at how to extend your melodies in sequences.

In harmony we'll first practise recognizing chords by their sound and how to join them together with good inner lines. We'll explore the sonority of different voicings. And we'll learn how to enrich harmony by using extensions and chords like the diminished chord.

Thus armed, we can then in the next three chapters explore three distinctive jazz harmonic styles: (1) bebop II–V–I harmony, used in standards and other mainstream tunes; (2) modal harmony, which stretches back to Western plain-chant and embraces many forms of World music; and (3) the harmony of the blues—a central jazz style since its inception, and using its own characteristic scale and chords. You'll find that jazz musicians continually make use of all *three* approaches, sometimes within the same bar; we've only treated them separately here to make them easier to learn. As you'll see, they overlap, and are really three different ways of seeing the same process.

Melodic vocabulary

Intervals

Developing an awareness of intervals, the gap between two notes, is a vital aural skill, and is tested specifically in the syllabus aural tests at Grades 4 and 5. By appreciating the characteristics of intervals, you will come to understand melody and harmony.

Let us begin by looking at intervals in melodic work. One way to make your melodies interesting is to choose a wide variety of melodic shapes. The interval is the building block that makes this possible. In the early stages, you can shape the character of your improvisation simply by choosing whether to use stepwise movement or wider leaps. Later on, this will lead into more focused exploration of the precise differences between, for example, major and minor 3rds and their use in particular modal contexts.

Activities

1   To explore the use of intervals in more detail, begin by inventing a vamp of your own, or choose a simple one from the selection in the Appendix, for example, this:

Choose a suitable mode or scale from a piece you are working on and make up an improvisation over this vamp. Make it between two and four bars long, and use only stepwise movement (you'll find that your scale practice helps you to move quickly in steps up and down the keyboard). In this case, we will limit the range to the first five notes of Mixolydian on C:

Keep on repeating the vamp while you investigate the intervals between these five notes. Start with the smallest, the semitone (E–F), and work round to the other notes. Try them ascending and descending, or mixing as you like, working through all the possibilities to discover new ways to make lines.

2   Now use the same vamp and scale, but this time use the whole scale in all the octaves of the instrument, and use intervals not smaller than a 4th. Be as outrageous as you can, and perhaps listen to a bit of Thelonious Monk for inspiration. Start very low down, or very high up, using the whole range of the instrument, and stick to the rules—nothing smaller than a 4th.

Listen to the CD. How did the two approaches sound different from each other? Are there some ideas that you can use in your own work? Obviously, these are two extremes, designed to make a point—most of your improvisations will fall somewhere between the two. But these activities demonstrate the range of what is possible.

3   Now go again, using mostly stepwise movement, but allowing the odd surprising leap. Notice how effective and unexpected this can be.

4   Play four bars of stepwise moves then four contrasting bars of leaps. Repeat the exercise, starting this time with leaps.

5   Invent more lines, based on other intervals, or perhaps concentrating on one interval in particular—a major 3rd, a 6th, a 5th. Some players use one section of their improvisation to accentuate the sound of 3rds and 6ths within a given mode, then explore 2nds and 7ths in the next. You can reflect these changes of emphasis in the chords and voicings you use.

Types of interval

In Chapter 3 we categorized 3rds and 7ths as major or minor, depending on whether the note was raised (major) or lowered (minor). We can classify 2nds and 6ths in the same way. When 4ths and 5ths appear in their usual diatonic form they are called 'perfect'. These intervals can also be 'diminished' (lowered by a semitone) or 'augmented' (raised by a semitone). The most common forms are diminished 5th and augmented 4th (one and the same thing, also known as a 'tritone'); this is an important interval in the blues scale.

We could summarize these intervals as follows:

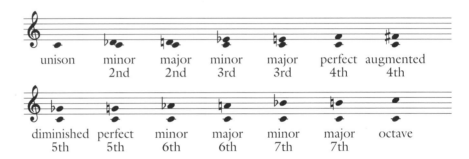

There's another important way to categorize intervals, based on their *sound*. Compare these two improvisations over the same root, both in Mixolydian mode. Notice the bracketed intervals in each case.

You will have noticed that intervals differ from each other in character. Some sound smooth, which we call *consonant*; others sound harsher, which we call *dissonant*. We can divide all intervals into these two categories, consonant and dissonant.

Look again at the main interval from example (*a*) above. This interval is a 6th—the first two bracketed intervals are major 6ths; the third is a minor 6th. It sounds smooth and rounded, whether played melodically or as a chord. It is a consonant interval.

Compare this with the main interval from example (*b*):

This interval is a 7th—a minor 7th in the case of the first two bracketed intervals, a major 7th for the last. Melodically, the 7th makes a wide and angular leap; harmonically, a 7th sounds harsher. We classify it as a dissonant interval.

With any interval we can play the lower note of the pair an octave higher, so that the interval changes. This is called inversion. If we invert a 6th we get a 3rd; if we invert a 7th we end up with a 2nd:

Unsurprisingly, 3rds have a smooth sound like 6ths, and 2nds and 7ths similarly share a harsher sound.

Finally, let's look at 4ths and 5ths (one an inversion of the other). Perfect 5ths are generally thought of as consonant but 'open', though in some situations, as we have seen, the 4th can be a dissonance (see Chapter 3).

Activities

1 As an exercise in understanding levels of dissonance with the root, let's look at the scale of Dorian on G. Play each note in turn against the root, and identify those which you think are more dissonant and those which are more consonant:

2 Make up a simple vamp and improvise melodic lines based on these various intervals. Listen to the contrasting sounds of the consonant and dissonant intervals.

3 As you play, explore the principle of inversion. For example, take a major 3rd, C to E; now invert it, playing the C an octave higher to make a minor 6th:

Invent a short improvisation focusing on these three notes, C, E and the C above, over our vamp from earlier. Notice the effect that inverting intervals has on the melodic line. Notice also how inverting an interval changes it from major to minor, or vice versa. Do the same with another pair of intervals.

4 Now try improvising over a vamp of your choice. First of all only use more consonant intervals and their inversions, and then only using more dissonant ones. Consider the contrasting effect each has, all within one mode.

5 Next, identify from the first five degrees of a scale which note will provide the most dissonance. Is it the 2nd?

6 Improvise over a bass-line, using only perhaps consonant notes until a given signal, then only dissonant ones. Once the ear is fully aware of the difference, mix the two.

In practice it is hard to generalize about the roles particular intervals take, as so much depends on context. However, you should get to the point where you can distinguish between 3rds and 6ths, and 2nds and 7ths, by ear. Track 54 plays each interval, first separately as two notes and then as a chord: listen to this until you can recognize each. Focus on each in turn, and learn the sound by using them in improvising and by singing what you play.

Added notes

In Chapter 3 we saw how you can use the triad tones to make melodies. Once you feel comfortable using these, you can begin to add extra notes to your triadic chords to make them sound richer and more dense.

Here are the first 8 bars of 'Barrelhouse Blues' by Tim Richards (Grade 3):

Notice how the chord in bars 1–2 is G major and in bars 5–6 C major. Try playing the example just with the triad shapes, i.e. using B, D and G in bars 1–2 and E, G and C in bars 5–6. Now add in the extra 6th in each case and listen to the difference. The second version is more idiomatic, particularly for 1930s and 1940s swing playing. Sometimes you will see the chord written as G6 or C6 (as here).

Now look at the second bar of Roland Perrin's 'Saturday' (also Grade 3):

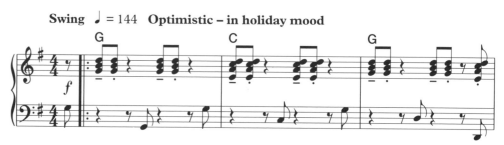

Notice the added 6, the A, and also the added 9, the D, which stays at the top of the texture throughout these bars.

When you are preparing your pieces at Grades 3–5, think about which triads in the solo section and perhaps even in the head could be made thicker with an added 6th, 7th or 9th. These rich chords are very much part of the sound-world of jazz and can make a piece sound great, used sparingly.

Chromatic neighbour notes

Here is another simple device you could try to embellish the triad notes. Chromatic neighbour notes are those a semitone above or below a chord note. To construct a line with chromatic neighbour notes, first write a phrase using the chord notes only, such as:

Then add the notes a semitone above or below the chord notes, for example:

Colouring the important notes of a melody in this way, by adding semitone embellishments can be used to add harmonic tension and interest to melodic phrases in the right hand and to left-hand walking basses. 'Blue Monk' (Grade 4) is a good example of a tune which uses this kind of chromatic movement and dissonance. Practise your chromatic scales to learn how best to make use of these ideas.

Melodic sequences

Having established the particular character of your melody, by using consonant and dissonant intervals and added notes, you now need a way of developing it. We are going to look at the technique of sequence, which involves repeating the phrases of your melody at different pitches and at different places in the bar. Let's suppose your melody uses the interval of a 6th:

We can now extend the melody by repeating it one note higher in the mode:

or up a 4th or 5th:

If your phrase starts, for example, on the 5th of the chord, try starting it again on the 5th of the next chord, like this:

These are all good examples of motivic work, where the melodic character of an initial idea or motive is preserved but extended. See the section on 'Developing your improvisation' in the previous chapter for more ideas on using a motive, particularly rhythmic ideas.

Choosing the pitches

We looked above at dissonant intervals, and saw how using these in our melodies created more angular tunes. We can also choose melody notes which are dissonant with the underlying harmony.

Let's set up a simple groove in C. First here is a four-bar solo which concentrates on the notes C, E, G and A, making consonant intervals with the C in the bass:

Here it is again, but this time with a solo which focuses on the pitches B♭, F and D, notes which are dissonant with the bass:

Improvising with the blues scale makes you very aware of this type of dissonance, as the flattened 3rd and 5th clash with the often major underlying harmony. Here's a typical example using the blues scale on C:

Nevertheless the dissonant ♭5 and ♭3 of the blues scale can sound good in major-scale contexts. And the semitones between the 4th and 5th degrees of the scale provide an exciting diversion from the brighter, more consonant sound of the major pentatonic scale.

Harmonic vocabulary

In Chapter 3 we learned to recognize chords by the intervals they contain, for example by recognizing the major third in a major chord, or a flattened 7th in a 7 chord. Let's now take this recognition process further.

Identifying chords

When you're actually improvising, there is often no time to work out what individual chords sound like by listening for each note in turn. Instead, most musicians develop another kind of listening, one that involves hearing a chord as a single sound, and identifying it by its 'colour'.

Activities

1   Listen to the following 1, 3, 5 chords, leaving out 7ths for now. Try to identify each immediately as either major or minor by the colour of the whole sound. To help you, the 3rd is at the top of each chord. Use your intuition and try to make an instant decision. Make mistakes if necessary, but avoid trying to identify or sing the 3rd in your head:

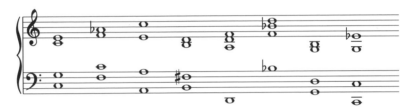

Can you tell whether the chord is major or minor by its whole sound alone? If you get some wrong to begin with, don't worry. Go back and do some more work on the intervals individually if you need to.

2   Once you've mastered 1, 3, 5 chords, add the 7th, and repeat the exercise until you can identify the four main 7th chords by their colours: 7, maj7, m7, m maj7. Have a go at these, but be careful—the 7th isn't always on top:

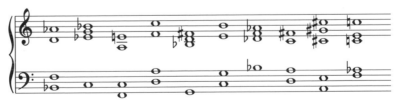

3   If you've bought one of the Board's graded CDs which accompanies each grade of the syllabus, choose a piece you don't know and listen to the performance of it, trying to work out the changes. Check back against the printed edition.

4   You can also try making up little improvisation exercises for yourself, to help you hear a particular change. In the next example, you should be able to hear clearly a change from major to minor and from major 7 to 7, over the same root.

Using only notes 1, 2, 3 and 5 of the scale, of which only the 3 needs to change, try improvising over these alternating chords:

5   When you can do this, try replacing Cm7 with another chord such as F7:

Notice the move from B♮ to A and from E to E♭. Sing it to yourself. You can see that this is a good way of integrating your aural training into your improvising. You learn a new sound by singing it and then playing it through. All the kinds of chord used in the following sections ideally need to be learnt aurally as well as in the fingers, and you'll find the technique of hearing a chord as a whole sound works better than always having to work through each interval one by one.

Inner lines

Once you can confidently identify a chord by its sound and can choose the chord to use in a particular context, you need to think about joining chords together and the importance of inner lines.

In Chapter 4 we saw how the guide tones (the 3rd and the 7th) created smooth lines guiding the harmony in a II–V–I progression. If we examine the position of each note in these chords, we find that the 7th and 3rd swap positions from one chord to the next. For example, in the first chord of a II–V–I in C, the 7th of Dm7 (C) is below the 3rd (F), whereas in the second chord (G7) the 3rd (B) is below the 7th (F). The 3rd of Dm7 becomes the 7th of G7 (they're both F), and the 7th of Dm7 (C) moves to the 3rd of G7 (B).

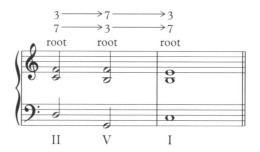

The same thing happens between G7 and Cmaj7. Each time, the 7th moves to the 3rd and the 3rd to the 7th, in a regular sequence.

Activities

1 Look at the inner lines in the following progression:

Play it through, and sing the inner lines. Listen to it played on track 57.

2 Now try singing the notes of each chord in order, from the lowest note to the highest, like this:

The best way to learn a chord sequence is aurally, like this. Writing the elements of the chords over each one, as we did above, will remind you of the movement. Once you've got these inner lines in your head, you can consider which voicings to use.

3 Try the longer sequence again, this time in B♭:

Voicings

If you sat at the keyboard and played the chords of a II–V–I progression in C in their raw triad form, they would sound like this:

To begin with, it is useful to have the chords set out in this way, so that the basic shapes can be easily understood. But if you played the chords like this in an improvisation, say an octave lower in the left hand, the effect would be stodgy and unstylish. So we use the guide tones against the root, which, as we've just seen, creates good inner lines, and also gives you a simple yet idiomatic set of voicings.

Most jazz and blues players make use of various kinds of voicing. The same chord can be made to sound different depending on how the notes are arranged vertically and how they are spaced. Some players add extra notes to chords for the sake of a richer or more colourful sonority. Also, different jazz styles demand different ways of voicing the same chord, and even within the same piece, a player may need to alter the voicing when there is a solo, say, or when the dynamic changes.

Activities

1   Let's begin with our simple three-note voicing. Once you have established the initial root and 7th position in your left hand, add the opposite guide tone with the thumb of your right hand and realize the II–V–I progression, like this:

2   Another approach is to play all three notes in your left hand, perhaps by spreading the chord like this:

3   or by alternating the bass-line and chord in what is essentially a two-part texture, like this:

This example is characteristic of the popular jazz-piano style called 'stride', where the left hand is continually striding up and down the keyboard, alternating between the bass and the chord. This 'um-cha' sound gives great rhythmic impetus to much jazz piano in swing styles, and was perfected by pianists like Art Tatum and 'Fats' Waller.

4   Now let's use all four notes of the chords, 1, 3, 5 and 7. Firstly, here are the notes bunched up closely, the so-called closed position. The sound is very thick:

5   Contrast that with the open position, where there is more space between the notes and as a result the sound is fuller and richer:

6   Finally, let's omit the root altogether and simply *imply* it, as though there were a bass player playing along with you. The listener's ear will often allow you to leave the root out, so that you can play the 3rd and 7th or 3rd and 5th. Here is the same sequence played with 3rds and 7ths:

58   Listen to all these different voicings on track 58.

7   As a last point in our discussion of voicings, remember that some styles of jazz are more triadic in sound, and the 7th is restricted only to particularly expressive moments. Chris Batchelor's 'Heading Home' (Grade 4) is related to the vocal harmonies of gospel music, and so predominantly uses 1, 3, 5 voicings:

You can hear that voicings are an expressive device in their own right and add character to the sound. Experiment at the keyboard with different voicings and try to recreate the simplest voicings from jazz recordings you particularly like. Look at the voicings in the pieces you are learning: how else could you voice those chords? Are there other voicings you prefer? As always, your ear and personal taste should be your guide. Aim to keep the inner lines clear and practise playing the same sequences in different keys.

Extensions

Once you understand the principle of guide tones and can make voicings using 3rds, 5ths and 7ths that make good inner lines, you can begin to add extensions to your chords. Extensions are notes which add extra dissonance and richness to the chord, and yet act in some ways according to the rules of functional harmony. Extensions are usually named using numbers above 8 and are most frequently referred to as the 9th, 11th and 13th.

Let's take a chord of C7 and add in the extensions. Firstly, here it is with an added 9th:

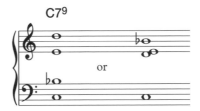

Now here it is with an added 11th, in this case a sharp 11th, and with an added 13th:

Notice that the extension, if it is indicated in the chord symbol, is written above it, slightly to the right. Go through these new chords again for practice, this time based on F7, G7, D7 and B♭7.

Activities

1 Here are some examples of how these chords work at cadences. These are all decorations of a V–I cadence, using simple voicings as a basis. Play each in turn and sing the top line.

The 9th can be natural (diatonic to the scale), flattened or sharpened:

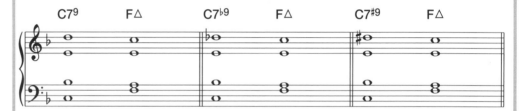

The 11th can be natural or sharpened:

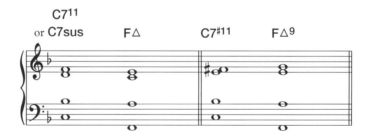

and the 13th can be natural or flattened:

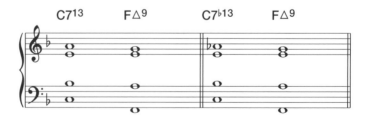

2 Invent a right-hand melodic phrase which uses the given extension. Play it with these different voicings.

In all of these cadences the extensions move with the guide tones. Notice how in each case the extension also resolves, usually to another extension or the next nearest note by step, so that the texture is kept even, just as with the guide tones.

It is helpful here to divide the extensions into two groups, with the 9ths on one side opposite the others:

♭9   9   ♯9   11   ♯11   5   13   ♭13

In the example above of a 9th, notice how the D resolves to a C—a 9th to the 5th of the next chord. In the example with a sharp 11, the 11th resolves to the 9th of Fmaj7, as do the 13ths. A general rule emerges that any note in the left-hand group normally resolves to any note in the right-hand group, and vice versa. (The 5th is included in the right-hand group as a possible note of resolution for the 9th.)

Notice in the above example that the natural 11th does not occur with the major 3rd, but occurs without it as a sus(4) chord. In a cadence, the 11 on chord V is usually *only* found as sharpened, since the natural 11 (F in this case) is the home note of the key and its use would clash with the 3rd of chord V; it would also prevent chord V from sounding unresolved. Similarly an 11th added to chord I would clash with the 3rd of that chord a semitone away and would reduce the sense of cadential resolution. So avoid using the natural 11 *and* the third in the same chord in V–I sequences.

In the materials accompanying this syllabus, and particularly in the books of pieces, we have tended to omit marking extensions in the changes, in order to make the charts clearer to follow and to put the emphasis firmly on making good lines with 3rds and 7ths. Generally, you'll only find extensions marked for more exotic final chords to pieces or where the music is particularly rich or chromatic. (We *do* mark extensions more freely in the books of aural tests, in order to introduce them, yet within a book which will be used mostly by teachers.)

But extensions are present in the voicings and notes used, and it's worth taking the time to explore the richness and variety that you can add to the harmony with extensions. As with many such effects, less is more: one extended chord used at the right moment can have a greater impact than strings of them used without thought. When you feel ready, get as much experience of using them in your playing as you can, as they are very much part of the style.

Chord inversion

In most cases in jazz the bass note will be the root of the chord; this is by far the most common use of chords across many styles of jazz. On some occasions, however, the bass note of a chord can be the 3rd of the chord:

C7/E

This is called first inversion and in Roman numerals is labelled Ib. You may also find it labelled using the 'triad over bass note' method, as here (more on this in

Chapter 10). The first inversion is often used as a passing chord, i.e. a chord 'passing' between two stronger chords, for example like this:

The bass note can also be the 5th of the chord:

This is called second inversion, and in Roman numerals is labelled Ic. This chord is most often found over a pedal, sometimes alternating with chord V:

Play chords on C, F, G, D and B♭ roots in root position, first and second inversion, and find examples of inversions in the pieces you are learning.

Unlike classical harmony, it is comparatively rare to use chord inversions as part of the underlying harmony in much of jazz. Instead, complexity in the bass-line harmony is provided by the walking bass-line or stride bass, both of which in a sense continually use different inversions as they march up and down the chord tones and scales. As a player, though, you'll be concentrating on making a good walking bass-line, adding chromatic notes and moving smoothly between the changes, or on a lively stride bass pattern, or on using the guide notes without roots for the sound of the voicings, rather than consciously using a particular chord in a particular inversion.

Diminished and half-diminished chord

An important chord to add to your harmonic repertoire is the diminished chord, which is formed by stacking minor 3rds on top of each other. Its chord symbol consists of the note on which it's based, with a small circle placed to the right:

You could also think of it as a chord containing the flat 3rd, the flat 5th, and the *double* flat 7th:

The diminished chord has many uses, most notably as a passing chord. It is often used as a means of passing from chord IIm7 to chord I, as follows:

Notice the rising bass-line and the first inversion chord, C/E. Similarly, it is found as a passing chord between chords IV and V, again with a chromatically rising bass-line:

Finally, it appears in this over-used jazz-piano cliché which ends many pieces:

60 These examples are played on track 60.

┌─ **Activities** ─────────────────────────────────────

1　Find diminished chords on different roots and practise voicing them at the piano.

2　Play the sequences above in various common keys. Try the ending one, but don't use it too much!

└───

The *half-diminished* chord consists of the flat 3rd, the flat 5th and the flat 7th (it's this last note which thus distinguishes it from the diminished 7th). The symbol for the half-diminished chord is a circle with a slash through it, placed to the right of the bass note:

Keys

Finally, let us turn briefly to the concept of key. We might speak of a blues in G; we recognize that standards are in particular keys and that modal pieces are built around key-notes and modes which determine the harmony. Chords and scales are often related through this concept of key, which defines not only which chords may be used in any one context, but also defines their hierarchy, within which each chord has its own particular function.

In Chapter 3 we built triads on each degree of the major scale. Let us now build 7ths on each:

All of these are diatonic to the key of C, that is to say they use only the notes of the scale of C major. You can play these, and work them out for yourself in other keys, simply by making a 1, 3, 5, 7 shape with your hand and placing it on each degree of the scale in turn (remember the sharps and flats for each key!).

Look closely at the types of 7ths formed. Two degrees of the scale, I and IV, produce major 7 chords; one degree (V) produces a 7th chord; and there are three degrees where minor 7 chords are built—II, III and VI. The chord built on the 7th degree is a half-diminished chord.

You will be familiar with all these different kinds of 7th chords, and you have learnt to recognize and use them. Knowing how they relate to the key, and understanding the scales and modes built from them, enables you to explore the melodic and harmonic possibilities of each key to the full.

Chapter summary

○ Identify common *intervals* and use a wide variety of them as you make melodies.

○ Classify intervals, as *major* or *minor*; *perfect*, *augmented* or *diminished*; *consonant* or *dissonant*.

○ Extend your melodies with *chromatic neighbour notes*; develop them with *sequences*.

○ Choose pitches which are consonant or dissonant with the underlying harmony.

○ Identify complete single chords by their sound.

○ Join chords together smoothly by using *inner lines*.

○ *Voice* chords in different ways to create a range of sonorities. Contrast *closed position* with *open position*; play through the changes using *stride*.

○ Enrich your harmony using *added notes, extensions* and the *diminished chord*. See how these chords resolve and join smoothly with the guide tones and surrounding chords.

○ Recognize chords in *first* and *second inversion*.

○ Understand the concept of *key*, and discover how chords and scales are related through a key.

Chapter 9 Playing Standards

Jazz tunes are great vehicles. They are forms that can be used and reused. Their implications are infinite.

LEE KONITZ

Jazz standards are tunes that have become classics. They form a core repertoire that musicians play regularly all over the world. As you learn the standards, you are becoming part of the whole jazz culture. You will know that you can walk into a strange club or rehearsal room anywhere and start into a standard. Everybody will join in, playing the same chords, in the same key, as if by magic. Jazz players all know their standards!

The tunes are often taken from popular music. Many of them come from the great age of Broadway shows, between the 1930s and 1950s, though the repertoire continues to grow. They become established as standards because they are particularly beautiful, challenging or simply fun to improvise around. They usually have a strong melody, and a common chord sequence that gives plenty of scope for improvisation. In the harmonizations found in jazz, many of them use II–V–I progressions, though standards with more elaborate changes have come into the repertoire. Some tunes that started out with different harmonies had them reharmonized into II–V–I sequences by jazz players themselves. We will look below at one of the commonest progressions, based on Gershwin's standard 'I Got Rhythm'. The sequence is known as Rhythm Changes.

The structure of standards usually follows common jazz patterns. Many of the tunes we have looked at so far are in so-called 32-bar song form. An eight-bar tune or phrase is played twice, is followed by a middle eight or bridge, where the harmony and melody changes for eight bars, and the song ends with a return to the opening tune. This is sometimes called AABA form, with the B standing for the middle eight. Many standards are in swing time or moderately slow ballad time.

Harmony

By learning standards you are getting used to common chord progressions and finding ways of dealing melodically with tricky harmonic problems. 'Christopher Columbus' and the Sonny Rollins tune 'Oleo', for instance, both use a variation of Rhythm Changes.

The middle eight of 'Christopher Columbus' contains a sequence of inversions of 7th chords:

Here it is again with the roots added. These descend by a 5th each time (or, in their inversion, ascend a 4th):

Sing the bass-line and play the voicings until you can recognize it instantly whenever you come across it.

Modulation

In Chapter 8 we looked briefly at the idea of a key. Keys can change during a piece, in a process called modulation. Most standards modulate at some point, often in the middle eight. When the new key is confirmed by a V–I cadence, the modulation is said to be complete. If the new key is used for only a bar or two, with a less definite cadence, it is known as a transitory modulation.

Activities

Let's look at the middle eight of Charlie Shavers' 'Undecided' (Grade 4) and plan a suitable improvisation over the chords.

1   The key of the tune is B♭ major, so begin by playing this scale.

2   However, the middle eight (section B) starts with the following chords (here are the guide tones):

Fm7 and B♭7 contain the note A♭, which is not in the scale of B♭ major. The V–I cadence is now in E♭ major, B♭7 to E♭△. This is a modulation, so in your improvisation you could use notes from the scale of E♭ major over this sequence. Play the scale of E♭ major.

3   Play the guide tones and notice how the inner lines descend smoothly, A♭–G and E♭–D.

4   Now let's think about the right hand. The difference between the two keys is that A♮ becomes A♭, so you could point up the modulation by concentrating on A♭, while following the inner lines. Here is one possibility:

Play this one with the guide tones and then invent one of your own.

5   The next four bars have the same progression, this time leading towards a cadence in F major. Here are the guide tones:

This time the scale to use is obviously F major. Our available pitches for the new key now include A♮ and E♮, rather than A♭ and E♭. Play the scale of F major.

6   F7, as we know, is chord V in B♭ major, the key of the A section. So the F7 is preparing us to return to the main key at the end of the eight bars. Your improvisation could go like this:

Play this one and invent one of your own.

7   Write out the chart for the whole middle eight, adding in the chord symbols and the scales identified above.

In the exam pieces you are given guideline pitches. You don't have to work out each scale before you play. But playing randomly from each scale won't give any sense that the melody and harmony are working together. You should be able to select pitches that not only fit the harmony but emphasize the movement of the chords.

Here are two further examples of melodic lines over these changes. The first again emphasizes the important notes which alter to signal the modulation:

The second adds movement using scales and arpeggios. It hints at the first modulation by using A♭ as a chromatic neighbour note in the first bar, and points the move back to B♭ major by reintroducing the note E♭ in the last two bars:

Before you play a piece, look through the changes and the melody for tell-tale signs of cadences. There may be V7–I△ progressions, often with the roots in the bass-line moving by a 5th. Or there may be melodic shapes that move from notes 7 to 1. Note 7 is called the leading note, because it commonly leads to the key-note. Also look for modulations or changes in the mode. Make good use of these moments in your melodies and voicings.

Turnaround

A turnaround is a progression that comes at the end of one chorus and which leads smoothly into the next. This is a typical progression:

I   VI   II(m)7   V

Here are the changes for the first eight bars of the Duke Ellington Band's 'Take the 'A' Train' (Grade 5). In bars 7 and 8, the chords form a I–VI–II–V progression.

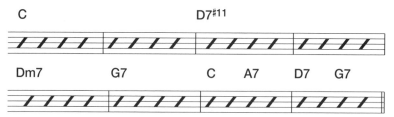

Here are the guide tones for the last four chords:

Activities

1   Play the scales implied by these chords:

2   In an improvisation, you won't want to play the entire scale every two beats! Instead, concentrate on the area of the keyboard where the pitches change. Take five notes: C, D, E, F and G. Look how these change as the chords change, and play each group of notes in turn above a left-hand voicing.

As you can see, the action centres on the C and the F. A7 sharpens them both; D7 returns the C♯ to C♮; then G7 restores the F♯ to F♮.

3   Improvise lines which show this movement, for example:

4   Now try lines which *avoid* the changing pitches, and stick to D, E and G:

5   Try this line, which changes only the C:

6   Finally, try an approach which expresses the harmony using arpeggios instead of scales. Notice the smooth progression from A–G–F♯–F♮, as well as the upper line of C–C♯–C♮–B:

This version would have been less interesting if we had simply laid out each arpeggio starting on its root. Instead, they are used as the basis of a melodic line. Vary the line as much as possible. Lead from arpeggios into scales, for example:

As always, your own taste and judgement must guide you.

7   Now repeat the sequence round and round, and improvise on the turn-around using these ideas.

Putting it all together

Let's go through 'Take the 'A' Train' as a whole, reminding ourselves of what we have looked at in Chapters 7 and 8.

Structure

Always begin by looking at the routine of a piece. In the Board's book of Grade 5 pieces this one starts, after a brief introduction, with a standard 32-bar chorus: there is an eight-bar phrase, which is repeated; then a middle eight, and then a return to the first eight bars. This entire 32-bar chorus is then repeated as a solo. The head then repeats from the middle eight, and includes the final A section and the coda. The whole thing can be summarized like this (the section in bold type is the solo):

Introduction   A A B A   **A A B A**   B A   Coda

Each A section consists of the following eight bars (in the Board's edition the G7 is decorated with a preceding A♭7, which we'll ignore for now):

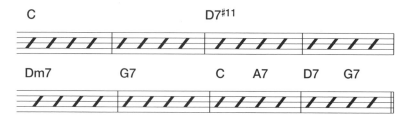

 Listen to the complete chorus on track 61 and note the AABA form.

Melodies

We should first examine the material to see what scales are implied by the harmony. As we saw above, deciding which are the most significant notes is the first step to deciding how to approach an improvisation.

Bars 7 and 8 are a turnaround. The first six bars are in C major, but with a twist—one of the chords has a note that doesn't belong to the scale of C major. It also has an extension, a note that adds colour to the melody and harmony.

Here are the roots and guide tones of the sequence:

The F♯ of the D7 chord does not belong to C major. It might suggest the key of G major or Mixolydian on D, both of which have F♯. But notice also that there is a sharp 11th, a G♯. If we make a scale out of the available pitches at this point, we have a very unusual scale. The way that it appears in the melody is wonderful:

Scale: Melody:

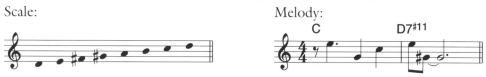

So the two unfamiliar notes up to the turnaround are the F♯ and G♯. These are the notes we should bear in mind when it comes to improvising around the tune.

Activities

1   Practise the scales suggested by each chord, beginning on the roots (we'll leave aside the turnaround, which we looked at earlier). Obviously, you won't want to play all these notes—a scale is not a melody—but by practising the scales you'll become familiar with the shapes and the notes which are altered:

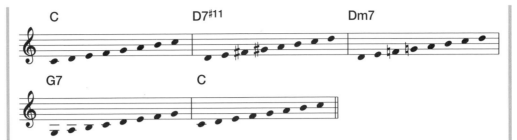

2   Think about the *key* and the importance of the key-note C. Since the chords of Dm7, G7 and C all contain the same notes, the tune at this point stays in C major. But the chord for bars 3 and 4 pushes away from C major. With complicated harmonies, your melody can wander, but it should still gravitate towards the key-note in the end. One way to keep track of this is to restrict the notes you can use from each chord's scale, or use only a pentatonic scale on each chord (notes 1, 2, 3, 5 and 7, occasionally adding 6).

3   As well as knowing which pitches you *could* use, you need to decide how many pitches you are going to emphasize. Will you concentrate on those that alter with the harmony? The F, for example, which moves to an F♯. Will you start with only two or three pitches and make a melody out of those? Or perhaps you'll choose the notes that are common to all the chords? You could invent a melodic shape, and then modify it to fit the harmony, perhaps starting with this:

and then repeating it, keeping the shape, but altering the notes to fit the movement of the harmony, like this:

4   If we started with the arpeggios appropriate to each chord, instead of the scales, we would have the beginnings of a further approach to the melody. Play straightforward arpeggios, using the root, 3rd and 5th, plus the 7th and extension if the chord has one:

As we found above with the scales, this in itself does not make an interesting melody! But it does get you used to the changes, this time by leaps rather than stepwise movement, and gives you the basis for further melodic shapes you might use.

5 Try playing through the guide-tone lines in turn. Think of ways in which you could embellish the line by using chromatic neighbour notes, anticipations, moving notes up an octave, and so on.

Take this sequence of guide tones:

and then the other:

Now invent a melody of your own that uses elements of both lines at different points.

The left hand

Begin by practising the possible chord shapes in your left hand. Remember your work on voicings in Chapter 8.

1 Start with full root-position triads and 7ths, to see the notes available, but remember not to play full chords like these in your improvising:

2 Now give the chords more clarity, thinning the chords and perhaps introducing a bit of stride:

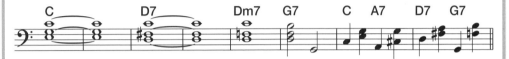

3 Think of the guide-tone shapes, using 3rds and 7ths:

4 Finally, remember that chords can be voiced using both hands:

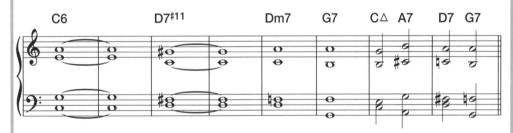

5 Once you have the harmony in your ears and good, musical shapes under the fingers, think about ways to enliven the left hand rhythmically, using vamps, rhythmic kicks, and all the other techniques we have practised.

Look carefully at the head, and see if there is any information that might start you off. Take the melody's rhythm in bar 2, for example:

It is strongly characteristic of the tune, and could be used as the basis of a repeated vamp, such as this:

Try not to make it too regular, though: the ear can tire of endless repetition!

Here's a suggestion for two eight-bar phrases, showing some of the techniques we have looked at.

62 Finally, track 62 gives three choruses of 'Take the 'A' Train', one with trio and with the piano comping, and then two with just bass and drums. Play along with the other musicians and try out some of the techniques and ideas you've been practising.

Chapter summary

○ Recognize and use the *32-bar song form* of standards and try to get a feel for the phrase structure, so that you no longer have to count the bars.

○ Identify common *chord progressions*, such as 'Rhythm Changes', and play them in various keys.

○ Identify *modulations* (often in the middle eight). Explore different sets of pitches for your right-hand improvisation which emphasize the modulation or, sometimes, which obscure it.

○ Play *turnarounds* in common keys and use these in your improvisations to move smoothly from one chorus to another.

○ When learning to play over a new standard, look carefully at the form. Practise scales and arpeggio shapes over the changes to learn the available right-hand pitches; and find the left-hand guide tones.

Chapter 10   # Using Modes

> We need to build up our confidence and learn to trust that there is something within us that can discover and perform from resources that go way beyond our conscious mind.
>
> BARRY GREEN

A mode is a particular kind of scale, used as the basis of a piece of music. From early Gregorian plainchant to North Indian Classical raga, improvisers and composers everywhere have used the rich possibilities of modes as an expressive tool. The early blues singers and players used modal inflections in their songs and tunes, notably the characteristic 'blue notes' (♭3, ♭5 and 7). What we call 'modal jazz' only emerged in the 1950s, in classic albums such as Miles Davis' *Kind of Blue*. At that time, jazz began to develop in a new and fascinating direction, as musicians experimented with improvising using modes as the basis for melodies *and* chords, *without* the strong sense of key that we worked on in the previous chapters.

The main characteristic of modal jazz is the exploration of the use of modal *colour* for its own sake—this chapter explains this idea in more depth later. Thinking outside the framework of a key and using modal colour creates new ways of playing. The opening of this new sound-world in jazz brought striking new melodies, chords and bass-line movements, and the modal approach remains a fertile way to improvise today, used by jazz musicians of all kinds.

The modes

In Western music, there is a special tradition of modes that came out of the medieval church and its plainchant. The church listed seven main modes and gave them names based on ancient Greek scales. For completeness, here are all the church modes. Notice that they use the same collection of pitches, in this case, the white notes of the piano, but they begin and end on different notes.

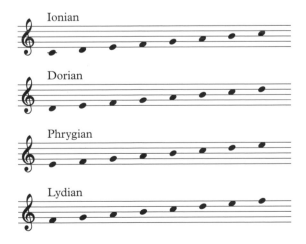

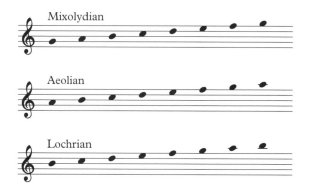

In this way of thinking, C major is the Ionian mode starting on C. It is one among seven equal modes, each with its own distinctive colour and expressive character, which comes from the arrangement of intervals in the scale. In modal jazz, each mode has its own separate and independent character.

Activities

1   Play each mode ascending and descending until you get the sound in your head. Keep playing the root of the mode in your left hand.

2   Now try playing each slowly in 3rds (C–E, D–F, and so on), then in 4ths (C–F, D–G), to get the sound of the intervals.

As you see, you can derive seven modes from these seven white notes. Of the seven named modes, we need to cover only *three* at Grades 1–5. These three are the Mixolydian, Dorian and Lydian. Remind yourself of how they sound, reiterating the root in the left hand as you do so.

Modal intervals

Music based on II–V–I harmony—tonal music—is based on the relationship of changing chords to chord I, the *tonic*. Other chords are thought of as more or less tense or relaxed as they move away from the tonic. In modal music, it is almost as if the tonic never goes away. It remains in the mind as a kind of drone, while melodies and harmonies change above it. Quite often the root actually *does* continue in the bass. Modal chord sequences often move more slowly than tonal ones, so we can begin by looking at modal improvising using only one root.

Because the root of the mode is thought of as always being present, the other notes have a more fixed relationship with it than in tonality. The interval between each note and the root, its consonance or dissonance, defines its place in the modal structure. It is important therefore to be able to recognize quickly the intervals from the root.

All the following examples are based around the Dorian mode on D.

A good way to check that you recognize the root is to practise resolving onto it.

1 Start with a simple bass-line, such as the one below. Play it through until you have it established. Then start to play a melodic line with the right hand, moving away from D for the first four bars, and back to D for the second four. Use only two or three pitches, perhaps like this:

2 Repeat the idea, but now aim towards a different target note, perhaps the fifth note of the mode, A. This time, reach the note by bar 3.

3 Now aim for the third, F:

4 When you get more advanced, try resolving also to the seventh (C), or even the ninth (E).

5 Now let's do the same, but this time using Mixolydian on D instead. Look at the difference between the two modes.

Notice that the difference is only one note. The F is now F♯, so the interval between the first and third notes is now a major rather than a minor 3rd.

6 Repeat the exercise as before, this time playing for four bars and using mostly F♯, G and A. After four more bars, resolve to D, perhaps using the odd C for variety:

Again explore resolving to the third, fifth or other degrees of the scale.

Did you get a sense of the very different colours of the two modes on D? It's amazing what a difference is made by changing only one note.

7 Now improvise over the following chord sequence, which contrasts four bars of Dorian with four bars of Mixolydian on D. Try also adding the notes A, B, C and the top D, which you'll notice are the same in both Dorian and Mixolydian on D.

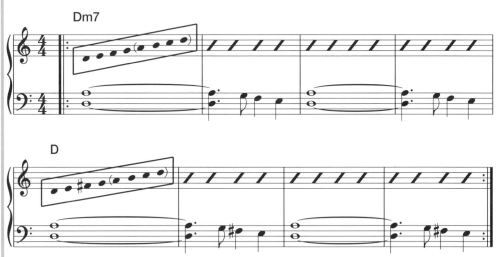

 8 Finally, listen to track 63 to hear the Dorian and Mixolydian modes contrasted. First hear chords based on them (listen to the F♮ and F♯ at the top), then a short improvisation using the bottom notes of the modes alternating in four-bar sections, and then an improvisation using the top notes of the modes in the melody and distinguishing the two modes in the harmony.

Interval patterns

Modes are distinguished from each other by the arrangement of the intervals, in particular the distribution of semitones. The church modes all contain two semitones, which appear between different degrees of the scale according to the mode. Because semitones are more dissonant than tones, it is these that give each mode its character.

The first semitone in the Dorian mode, for example, appears between the second and third degrees of the scale. In the mode on D, these are the notes E–F:

In the Mixolydian mode, the interval between the second and third degrees is a tone (E–F♯ in Mixolydian on D). The first semitone is between the third and fourth degrees (F♯–G):

The Lydian mode begins with three whole tones. The first semitone is now between the fourth and fifth degrees (on D, G♯–A):

Activities

1   Play and sing each of these modes, starting with just the first five notes. Learn to identify them instantly by their characteristics.

2   Using a simple bass-line like the one we have used before, play four bars of melody in each mode in succession. Emphasize the semitones.

The Dorian mode on D has two characteristic intervals: the minor 3rd (D–F) and the minor 7th (D–C). These define the range of possibilities for melodies and chords. It is the 'colour' of the mode, if you like; these are the intervals that occur in most music in the Dorian mode.

Taking the major scale (Ionian mode) and comparing it with the Dorian, Lydian and Mixolydian modes, the differences are these. The notes in parentheses are those that vary when the modes are based on D.

Dorian   ♭3 (F♯ becomes F♮)   ♭7 (C♯ becomes C♮)

Lydian   ♯4 (G♮ becomes G♯)

Mixolydian   ♭7 (C♯ becomes C♮)

These intervals are likely to be the focus of your aural and practical work at first. It is worth spending some time revising your work on intervals by listening to major and minor 3rds and 7ths and perfect and augmented 4ths, until you can recognize them at once and sing them back accurately.

Modal harmony

So far, we have thought of modes 'horizontally', in other words, about how their distinctive arrangements of intervals influence melodies. We can also think about modes 'vertically', that is, by the chords that they form.

1 Here are the two semitones in the Dorian mode on D. Play them against the root.

Notice the buzzing of the dissonances between E and F and between B and C. If your ear has problems picking them up, play them again separately.

2 Now play all seven notes together as a chord, with a strong D in the bass:

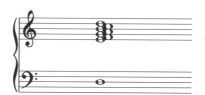

3 Do the same with Mixolydian on D, and you will hear that the dissonances have moved:

Miles Davis' 'All Blues' (Grade 5) is an example of a tune which moves from Mixolydian (on G) to Dorian (on G) and back again. See also pages 130–3.

4 The modes contain other significant intervals. For example, in Dorian on D, there is a major 6th between F and D. In the Mixolydian, this becomes a minor 6th. Listen to the difference between them over a D root.

Dorian on D   Mixolydian on D

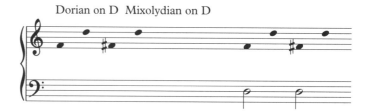

5 Now compare the Dorian and Lydian modes, this time on G. If you play the Dorian mode on G against a root in the bass, you'll probably notice how the minor 3rd (G–B♭) gives it a distinctly dark quality. The Lydian on G, on the other hand, has a brighter feel. It has a raised 4th (C♯) and a major 3rd (B♮).

These are differences not only in colour, but also in dissonance. Dissonance can also be thought of as tension which needs to be resolved. You can use this sense of tension in your improvisations.

Sonorities

In Chapter 9 we looked at how to use the distinctive pitches of each key to emphasize modulations. In the same way, we can use the unique interval patterns of modes to create sonorities particular to that mode. Some of these are conventional; others you can choose for yourself through careful listening and exploration.

We could start with the obvious shapes, the triads. These sound familiar and create consonances naturally.

They can also be inverted:

Modal jazz players often use other kinds of triads, including 1–2–5 and 1–4–5 shapes:

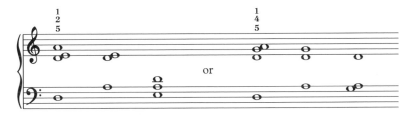

Here are some more advanced voicings for Dorian, Mixolydian and Lydian modes. Some are for both hands, some for only the left:

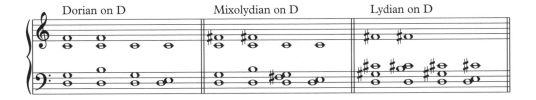

All contain only notes from their mode. Notice how some contain more dissonances than others.

Track 64 demonstrates some different voicings for Mixolydian on D in a short improvisation: first 8 bars of triads, then 8 bars of voicings including 7ths, and finally 8 bars using other sonorities from the mode.

Simple two- and three-note voicings work well at the early stages. As usual, concentrate on creating good movement with the roots and the guide tones. As you progress and become more confident, explore a wider range of chordal vocabulary, including 1–3–5, 1–2–5 and 1–4–5 shapes, with their inversions.

Modal tension

The level of dissonance plays a great role in shaping the character of your melodies. A melody that uses largely consonant intervals, such as 3rds and 6ths, against the root:

will give a very different effect from one which uses more dissonances, such as 2nds, 4ths and 7ths:

While remaining in the same mode, chords can include mostly consonances:

or dissonances:

This last example contains five notes, and many different elements of possible dissonance. Let's take it apart a little, and see what are the intervals that it makes. The root D is creating a rounded and consonant major 3rd with the F♯. There are also three different 7ths: D–C, G–F♯ and C–B:

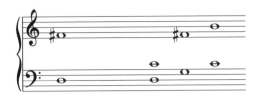

The result is a rich and resonant blend of sounds, with colours of great subtlety. Measuring the weight of dissonance in modal chords is crucial to understanding how they work, as we will see.

Modal inflection

We are by now used to the modal contrast between major and minor 3rds. But all intervals fall into these partnerships, and different modal contexts bring out the distinctions between them. There are minor and major 2nds, for example, sometimes written as ♭9 or ♮9, made from one or two semitones; perfect 4ths and augmented 4ths (sometimes written as ♯11); major and minor 6ths (sometimes written as 13 or ♭13); and major and minor 7ths. Modal jazz is full of these inflections.

Activities

Let's look at how they work. We'll take a familiar tune and transform it by moving it through our three modes.

1 Listen carefully to track 65 and notice which notes change as they are played in different modes. They are all on D: first Dorian, then Mixolydian and finally Lydian. In each case, we play the mode first. The tune, in case you hadn't noticed, is 'Three Blind Mice':

In your imagination, pick out the tune on your instrument as you listen. You may like to sing along. The changes will be very obvious from the start! Identify the notes that change. If you can, work out which note or which degree of the scale is different. Then try to play what you have just heard.

2   Invent your own examples, using tunes you know, and transforming them through different modes. As in the example, begin with something easy. Start by working them out by ear. Only write them down when you are sure you know how they should go.

3   Once this is an established game, repeat the whole tune using the three modes, but now on C. Notice the effect of the modal colour on the expressive character of the tune. Notice how it affects the fingering, too. Start with only a few notes from each mode, then move on to complete modes when you are ready.

Modal chord sequences

Modal chord sequences usually contain fewer chords than tonal or blues sequences. Typically, each chord lasts for a relatively long time, for four, eight, sometimes even 16 bars. A whole sequence can consist of only a couple of chords. For the improviser, this means that the only way to develop harmonic tension is by exploiting the levels of dissonance. Michael Garrick's pieces in the grade books show this in action very well.

Modal jazz gives more freedom than other styles when it comes to phrase length and form. That means that they can be used as directly expressive parts of the music. Chords that change very quickly will give a greater sense of movement. Variations in the speed of chord changes can set up tensions. So, for example, there could be a series of very quickly changing chords, followed by a section in which only one or two chords are used.

You can use asymmetrical patterns of phrases. A three-bar phrase could be followed by one of five bars, instead of the usual four-bar lengths. If you have worked through the exercises in earlier chapters, you should have developed an intuitive awareness of four-, eight- and 16-bar patterns. You should by now have an automatic sense of when they begin and end, without having to count the beats. Once you have achieved that, you are free to let the form breathe.

Chord changes

In longer mode sequences, there are sometimes chords that appear tonally unrelated to each other. Between the two chords there is a complete change of modal colour and voicing. It is up to the improviser to make the most of the difference between them. It could be that they want to emphasize the pitches that the modes have in common, or to make the most of the differences.

1   Let's look at how to use common pitches to move between modes. We'll start with two modes, Dorian on D and Lydian on E♭. To practise this, play the two scales and write them out on parallel staves, as here. Look at the keyboard, listen, and look at the notated scales, and identify those pitches which they have in common (F, G, A, C and D) and those which differ (E♭/E♮ and B♭/B♮).

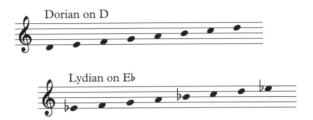

2   Play a simple chord sequence, using four bars of Dorian on D and four of Lydian on E♭. Invent a riff of one or two bars, containing only notes common to both modes—easy!

3   Now alter the chord to include one or two notes that change when the chords change. If you can, continue to improvise a melody above the chords. At first, use notes that are common to both modes, then those that change. Finally, use *all* the notes from both the modes.

Modal resolution

In tonal harmony tension is resolved by cadences in a key, usually using a II–V–I progression. In modal jazz there can be resolution without this sense of key. The tension and release is provided solely by the level of dissonance within the chords or melody. A tense and dissonant chord in the Mixolydian mode on G can resolve to a more consonant chord in the Lydian mode on E♭.

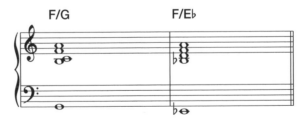

The tension and release are not tied to a home key.

To begin with, make use of dissonances in this way in a single mode. As you advance, you will get used to exploiting the expressive effect of intervals. You will be able to play chord progressions and fluent melodies as you move freely between modes.

Notation

Modal jazz can use the same system of chord symbols as other styles. It works well and is consistent.

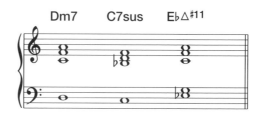

However, it can get cumbersome, especially when you need to notate extensions in the harmony. For this reason, players have developed a system called the 'triad over bass note' method. It doesn't necessarily give the literal voicing of the chord, but only the significant notes of a triad, above a root. It always shows the last significant semitone in the mode. The Lydian mode on E♭, for instance, is shown by an F triad, because it contains an A♮. Major triads are used in preference to minor triads. Below are voicings of the same chords, this time expressed in this way:

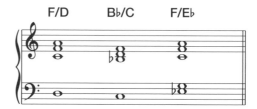

You are likely to meet both systems of notation. Many of our modal pieces use the 'triad over bass' method to indicate the chords in the improvisatory sections.

Putting it all together

Now let's try using these ideas in a modal piece. Here is the full modal chord sequence for 'All Blues' by Miles Davis, set out as in the book of Grade 5 pieces. Notice that it is a twelve-bar blues, with chord IV in bar 5 and chord V in bar 9. Count through the sequence, using the chord symbols to play the roots in dotted minims in your left hand.

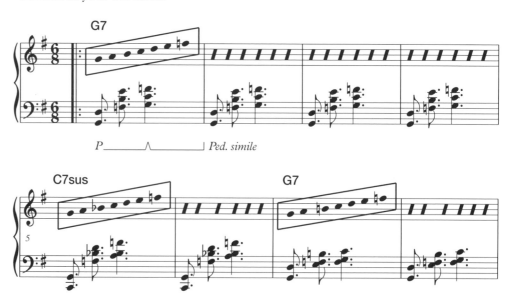

The right hand

Activities

1 Let's work on bars 1–4 first, just repeating the sound of Mixolydian on G. Remember that each pitch of the mode has its own sound against the root; some will sound more dissonant and some less. First try a line that emphasizes the consonant notes—root, 3rd and 5th—playing the root against each so that you can hear the difference:

Now one which emphasizes the more dissonant notes—9th, 11th and 13th:

2 Practise improvising four bars of one type (consonant or dissonant) followed by four of the other, or questions and answers that alternate both kinds.

3 Now try inventing a melody which floats above the root:

and then one which moves back towards it, resolving to it at the end:

4 Once the pitches of the mode are firmly in your mind, play around with the phrase lengths you use, to create and release rhythmic tension. Here are two contrasting ideas, first a regular four-bar solo built from a two-bar question and answer:

and now one consisting of more irregular phrase lengths, short and long:

Remember not to start all your phrases on the first beat!

5   Look again at the guideline pitches in bar 5. With the chord at this point a C7sus, these are best thought of as the pitches of Mixolydian on C, starting on the note G.* Play the first five notes of Mixolydian on G and the notes of Mixolydian on C starting from G and spot the note which alters as the mode changes:

One approach to improvising over these bars would be to signal the change of mode by using the notes B and B♭, like this:

Alternatively, you could use the pitches which *don't* alter, for example G, F, E and D, so that when the chord changes you can use the same pitches in bars 5–6 as you did in bars 1–4, like this:

6   You could build a solo from a repeated phrase which includes the note B, modally inflecting it to B♭ at bar 5:

Invent your own repeated phrase focused on B/B♭. The skill is to make the phrase identifiably the *same*, though one note changes.

7   You could use a motive which simply needs to be transposed into the new mode (up a 4th) when the mode changes from Mixolydian on G to Mixolydian on C:

8   Think also about the phrase lengths. You could register a change in mode by closing a phrase at the end of bar 4, where Mixolydian on G ends:

---

*These are, of course, the same pitches as Dorian on G.

Or you could play through the change and across bars 4–5:

The left hand

Let's now explore the range of possible voicings and sonorities available within the modes of Mixolydian on G (played in this tune over the G7 chords) and Mixolydian on C (played over the C7sus chords). As with the guideline left hand given, experiment with a texture which alternates a root or 5th with a higher voicing; play the root before each and use the pedal to make them sound together in a rich sonority.

Activities

1 Start off with triad shapes:

2 Now add the 7ths to make the guide tones, perhaps with some extensions:

3 Move the 3rd around, making 1–2–5 and 1–4–5 shapes in closed and open position:

4 Now add the 7th to make 1–4–7 voicings, like those used in the guideline left hand:

Notice how similar these voicings can sometimes sound, even though they are in different modes.

5 The given part predominantly uses these voicings. Notice how the F–B–E voicing in bar 1 is inverted to make an E–F–B voicing in bar 7; try inverting the other voicings given and those of your own invention to create open and closed shapes. Make up your own three-note voicings, using similar shapes but choosing any notes you like from the modes. Move up and down the white notes using these shapes and listen carefully to the different modal colours and sonorities which are made.

6 Listen also to tracks from Miles Davis' *Kind of Blue* album and pick out sounds you like—perhaps 8 bars of improvised melody or some voicings from the piano. Try including your favourites in your solo.

End of the sequence

Notice how bars 9 and 10, on chord V of the sequence, are perhaps the most tense of all, with the dissonant ♯9 voicing in the left hand rising by a semitone and then falling back.

Activities

1 Try playing a simple phrase in bar 9, and then raising and lowering it by a semitone in bar 10 to follow the harmony:

2 Finally, in the Coda think of ways of leaving more and more space, until the solo fades to nothing. How sparsely can you play?

Chapter summary

○ Understand the patterns of the seven *modes* and notice their different patterns of intervals.

○ Identify and use the *Dorian*, *Mixolydian* and *Lydian* modes. Note the differences and similarities in the intervals they make, particularly the position of the semitones. Examine the characteristic triads that are formed.

○ Explore the degrees of dissonance in modal intervals and chords. Notice how altering the weight of dissonance of chords generates tension and resolution.

○ Use *voicings* characteristic of each mode. Use the interval structure and vary the chord shapes to find sonorities that exploit different degrees of dissonance.

○ Notice the inflections that alter a melody played in different modes; play simple melodies in several modes.

○ Explore the opportunities for varying phrase lengths in modal jazz.

○ Use the different forms of notation in modal jazz, especially the *triad over bass note* method.

○ When learning a modal piece, identify the modes used and play them against the root. Explore different left-hand voicings. Choose different right-hand pitches, sometimes signalling the change of mode by emphasizing the notes which alter, sometimes playing across the change by using pitches common to both modes.

Chapter 11

The Twelve-Bar Blues

> When I was young I didn't understand that music came in sets of categories—music for babies, music for teenagers, music for old people, music for black people, music for white people. I thought it was all just music. We in the Western world suffer from too many categories and classes . . .We've separated music from life.
>
> ORNETTE COLEMAN

In Chapter 4 we looked at the basic form of the twelve-bar blues. Now we will begin to explore the style in more depth. We will find out how to use the blues scale to improvise over sequences, and look at some of the ways in which the twelve-bar blues has been varied.

Blues melodic style

The blues is a *vocal* style. In the early acoustic guitar and voice blues songs of musicians like John Lee Hooker, Howlin' Wolf and Big Bill Broonzy, the blues is characterized by expressive sliding between notes, perhaps not using pitches at all. Sometimes there is just the rhythmic speaking of words and a kind of intimate personal intensity of performance style, which comes from the telling of long stories, verse by verse, with long, rhythmically flexible solos. These solos rise to great climaxes and then fall back to the groove over very simple but rhythmically driving backings.

The blues as an instrumental form arises out of this vocal style, which features hollering, preaching, sighing and telling stories. It is this song-like, personal and intense vocal sound that players of all kinds try to recreate on their instruments. For pianists, it means a whole repertoire of ornaments, glissandos and accents and using characteristic pitches and scales.

The blues scale

Like the ♭3 pentatonic, the blues scale is actually little more than a convenient and easy way to get beginners to sound good playing the blues! Blues players themselves use any number of variants that are more subtle and interesting. The blues scale is a kind of simplified summary of real blues scales, but because it is common and recognizable, it's an important starting place for improvisation. Do remember to vary it though by substituting related scales, such as the minor pentatonic, ♭3 pentatonic and the Mixolydian mode.

Let's look at the blues scale and think about the notes it contains.

Minor 3rd

If we begin with the blues scale on C, the first note we encounter on the way up is E♭, the minor 3rd. It is sometimes called the 'blue' note, and is highly expressive. If you listen to one of the major gospel or blues singers, such as Bessie Smith, Mahalia Jackson and Aretha Franklin, the note they sing lies between the major and minor 3rd. On the piano, the note we want lies somewhere in the crack between E♭ and E! When we play a fast blues scale, the E♭ is often the right note. When we linger in a slow blues, we sometimes want to vary the note between E♭ and E♮, bright to dark:

4th, augmented 4th and 5th

These three notes form a little group on the way up the scale, and it may be helpful to think of them as forming a progression of tension. The 4th is more tense than the 3rd, the augmented 4th* more tense than the 4th, and the 5th is finally an arrival point. Harmonically, the 5th becomes consonant with the underlying harmony, but it is in a way more tense than the augmented 4th. Listen to this short solo as an illustration.

In a descending phrase, the augmented 4th and the 5th are sometimes used interchangeably. You might alternate them, in a kind of conversational variant.

7th

The 7th (B♭) is also at the heart of the blues sound. It reaches up to the tonic at the top of the scale, but is itself a blue note. As a blue note, it is tense and in need of resolution, either to the tonic or to the consonant 5th.

---

*The augmented 4th or diminished 5th can be thought of as an inflection of either the 4th or 5th, depending on the direction of the phrase. In jazz it is notated both ways, depending on which makes the chord or melody easier to read.

Hammering on

A blues melody in the right hand can be made more intense by adding a note at a crucial point. This is a gesture called 'hammering on':

becomes

This classic blues piano gesture can be overused, but it remains an important part of the language. Try also hammering on using other notes. You can expand the texture by adding thirds to the movement up and down the scale:

or by adding 6ths, either changing the shape of the melody, or in chords:

Strings of 4ths or 5ths are sometimes used to thicken and emphasize a melody:

Adding ornaments

Blues singers are able to use a wide range of articulations and deviations from pitch. They can slide around notes, add attack by using various consonants or clicks. Jazz saxophone or brass players can imitate this to some extent, using the tongue, diaphragm or reed.

With your voice, imitate a large brass section from an early Kansas City or Count Basie big band with the following sounds:

Wup!   Shoo-Bup!   Doo-Waah!

The opening consonant defines the *attack* of the sound. *Scat* singing uses these consonant sounds for expressive effects. With 'Shoo-Bup', for instance, you have a soft 'Sh' that leads into a hard 'B' and is cut short by the final '-p', like brass players abruptly stopping the air in the mouthpiece. These are common jazz gestures.

A pianist has fewer possibilities for defining the attack of a phrase. There are effects such as the swoop, where the player adds one or more chromatic grace-notes to the front of a note.

There is the slide or fall at the end of a phrase:

and the glissando over the whole keyboard, up or down:

These effects are best used sparingly, at moments of greatest intensity in a phrase. They can add character and importance to a gesture, like emphasizing a word in a song, but lose their impact if they are overused.

Blues solos

Blues solos are often long, dramatic and full of variety. Here are some common techniques to try.

Activities

1   Alternating registers in question and answer phrases:

2   Contrasting two registers:

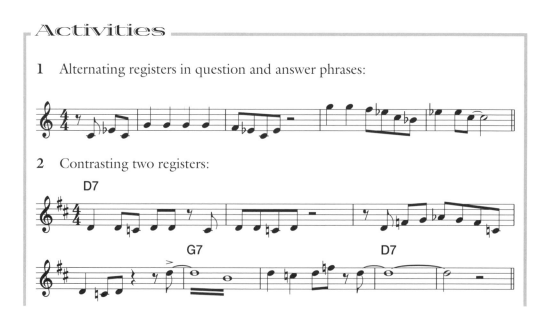

3 Building intensity by repeating a single recognizable phrase, while increasing the dynamics and varying the pitches and rhythms as you go:

4 Creating tension by playing one note repeatedly, apparently almost beyond endurance, before ending with a flourish.

5 Stopping the accompaniment to the solo, either in the first four bars:

or in the last one or two:

Listen to these various techniques demonstrated on track 66.

Breaks

'Breaks' appear in many jazz styles, but they are a particular feature of the blues. A break is a short solo melodic phrase that punctuates the music, usually while the accompaniment stops. It is often used to make a dramatic impact, or to launch a solo.

You can use short solos as breaks, before building them into longer solos. Breaks are found a lot in early jazz. Jelly Roll Morton used them widely, and they are perhaps the only really improvised parts of his recordings. Some of the syllabus pieces use breaks as well as more extended solos.

Try inserting a break in the bar before the solo in 'Lemon Cornette' (Grade 5). Play your opening solo phrase in the final bar of the tune, leaving out any left-hand part. Put in a stop in the first beat of bar 12, as we saw above.

Blues harmony

So far we have stressed the importance of working within the chord structure of a piece, while being as inventive and expressive as possible. In the blues, however, the player sometimes plays 'on top of' the harmony, using perhaps the simple blues scale throughout and seeming to *ignore* the harmony. Like most effects, this can be overused, but it does give an authentic sound.

The chord changes to G7, but the soloist carries on a blues scale in D regardless. It is more complex and jazz-like to alternate sections in which the improvisation converges with the accompanying harmony and sections where it plays apart. It can even get you out of situations where you lose your way!

With all these effects, it is best not to overuse the blues scale. It is very often more interesting and appropriate to use a *range* of scales and melodic devices. As usual, you must follow your intuition about what is needed in a piece. A good blues player will be able to draw tension out of a blues scale, but will be able to play through progressions and cadences when they are needed.

Blues voicings

The twelve-bar blues is such a universal phenomenon, that it is hard to make generalizations about voicings. You could use the styles of bebop or modal jazz, or you could explore the techniques of R'n'B piano.

The various forms of R'n'B, such as boogie-woogie and barrelhouse, started with such great piano players as Pine Top Smith, 'Cow Cow' Davenport and Meade 'Lux' Lewis in the 1920s and 1930s. The voicings are often based on simple but powerful 5ths or triads, rather than rich-sounding jazz voicings. For instance:

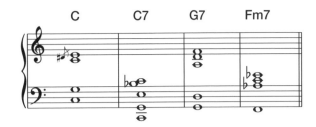

When 7th chords are used, they tend to be the 7 and minor 7s, rather than the sweeter sound of the major 7 and minor major 7. Moving from chord to chord very often involves sequences of warm 3rds or 6ths, either within a key:

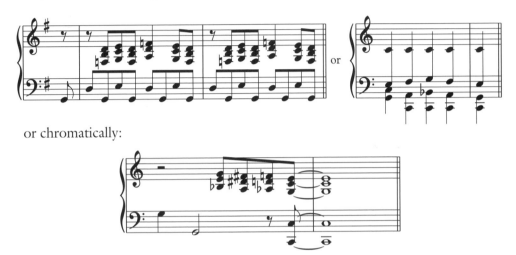

or chromatically:

But perhaps the prototype blues chord is this 7#9 voicing:

This mixes the major 3rd and 7th from a 7 chord, with the minor 3rd that comes from a blues scale.

Variations and substitutions

Early blues developed in a very scattered way. In the first few decades of this century different styles grew up in almost every region of the United States. There were R'n'B, urban and country blues, together with all kinds of jazz variants. They had different forms and lengths, and it is difficult to say which is the 'real' original blues sequence. Most of them, however, are around twelve bars long, and they usually start more or less with chord I, change to chord IV by bar 5, and to chord V by bar 9 or 10. We became familiar with this basic sequence in Chapter 4.

In one significant variation, the first four bars are extended to eight. The player seems to be waiting to continue, making a kind of verse-chorus form. The four bars turn into an eight-bar verse, and the return eight release the tension that is created, in the manner of a chorus. The classic Willie Dixon number 'Hootchie Cootchie Man' is in this form.

In bebop and much post-1940s jazz the basic twelve-bar pattern is varied using *chord substitutions*. Chords are substituted in order to embellish the harmony, to add greater interest or tension, but sometimes to *simplify* the harmony, to strip it down to its barest essentials.

Here's a simple example, which stays on chord V in bars 9 and 10, before dropping straight to I, thus avoiding chord IV:

In this next example there are more substituted chords: chord IV in bar 2, which adds movement at the beginning, the II–V–I in bars 9–11, and chord V in the last bar, which provides a smooth return back to the start of the sequence:

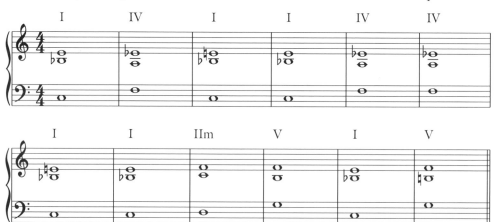

This substituted II–V–I progression is characteristic of blues played in the bebop era, when such progressions were added to create cadences at various points in the sequence. At the next level of complexity is a sequence like this one from Nikki Iles' 'Lemon Cornette', which uses the following sequence in the solo:

Here there is an extra II–V–I to B♭ in bars 4–5, a turnaround in bars 11–12, and the II–V in bars 9–10 is prepared with an extra D7, making a cadence onto Gm7. Note also the diminished 7th chord in bar 6, another characteristic substitution. This usually resolves up by a semitone to make a first inversion chord of chord I. Note, in this next example, the strong bass-line this creates:

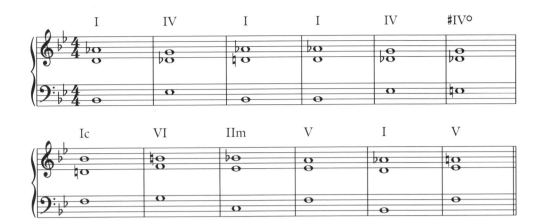

Duke Ellington's 'Things ain't what they used to be' uses this variant.

Finally, here is another, even richer version. Note all the substituted chords, and see how far the sequence has developed from the basic form!

Chapter summary

○ Familiarize yourself with and use the blues scale in common keys.

○ Explore the characteristics of blues melodic style, and use the expressive possibilities of the *blue notes*, the major/minor 3rd, the 4th/augmented 4th/5th and the flattened 7th.

○ Practise *hammering on*; add grace-notes and ornaments to embellish a line.

○ Learn what is meant by a *break*, and practise these short solo fragments. Use breaks as the starting-point for longer blues improvisations.

○ Use the chords and voicings of simple blues harmony. Use a continuing melodic blues scale over passages of changing harmony.

○ Use different *chord substitutions* to vary the basic pattern. Discover the richness of bebop substitutions.

Chapter 12 # Key Principles

The thing to judge in any jazz artist is does the man project, and does he have ideas?

MILES DAVIS

If this book has done its job, you will be well on the way to having the skills and experiences to play jazz and to learn for yourself in the future. This short final chapter of Part II draws together some of the main principles of the book and provides a framework for you to continue your learning by yourself.

In your practice

1 *Always warm up.* Every practice session should begin with rhythm exercises to warm you up physically and stimulate your sense of time. Clap, sing or click, tap your feet, snap your fingers to a backbeat. Loosen up your limbs, so that your mind and body are prepared to make music.

Listen to a jazz recording, relax and feel the groove. Echo rhythms you hear by clapping, matching the accentuation. Echo the notes your hear, singing nonsense or 'scat' syllables. Move straight into one of the pieces you are playing. Use the changes and groove of that piece to do the same kinds of exercise.

2 *Focus on the music.* Think carefully about the *style* of a piece, and what kinds of chords and lines are appropriate. Should you approach it with cadences, or using modal or blues scales? Is there opportunity for melodic or harmonic variation in successive phrases?

Begin to work at a tune by becoming familiar with its elements—its groove, melody and chords. Your playing will reflect how well you know these elements of a piece. It is impossible to be creative or stylish over a tune you don't *really* know.

3 *Make a diary of your regular practice time.* How much time do you spend on the following: warming up, technical practice, improvisation, learning repertoire, listening to other players and recordings, listening to yourself? Use your diary to make sure all these areas are covered properly.

4 *Note any physical tension.* When you play, become aware of any physical tension. Are you sitting straight? Are you able to move with the music? What happens to your body when you come to a particularly demanding passage? What happens when you come to a particularly *relaxed* passage? Develop a sense of physical ease, relaxed and alert.

5 *Note any mental tension.* When you play, become aware of mental tension. Which music do you particularly enjoy playing? Which do you find particularly difficult? What happens to your playing when you begin to worry about a particular piece? Take steps to ensure that your mind is clear and focused when you are improvising.

In your improvising

As you get more advanced as a player, the number of options open to you will increase, and you will get to know more music and become more technically fluent. This often leads to an overload of ideas, a phase many players go through where they try and put everything in, play as fast as they can or with real intensity. You get excited and feel able to communicate that excitement for the first time; perhaps you want also to compete or be impressive.

There are two undesirable extremes. At one is the player who plays safe, sticks to the chord tones and produces correct harmony, but whose playing lacks imagination and invention. At the other is the player who feels highly creative, energetic and inventive, but who has no grasp of the changes and perhaps is forced to play the blues scale throughout, ignoring the subtleties of the changes altogether.

Either way, at times like these it is more important than ever to remember the following:

1 *Leave spaces.* Silence makes each phrase sound good, and allows you time to consider what to play next.

2 *Keep it simple and clear.* Always begin with simple ideas that you can develop or elaborate. Many of the best improvisations begin with an idea that can be easily remembered by player and audience alike. Often the most impressive sounding and complex idea comes from the head rather than the heart. Could you get the same musical gesture across using fewer notes? Less is often more.

3 *Pace yourself carefully through long solos.* There is no point in finding yourself two bars from the end of an improvisation just as you are warming up; no point either in playing at the highest intensity for the first eight bars and be left with a long slow descent for the rest of the solo.

4 *Use contrasts to give your playing variety.* There is nothing worse than a one-solo jazz musician! Do you always play loud? Or always go for the high notes? Explore the full range of the musical resources you have: high and low, loud and soft, dense and sparse. Try and play in the style of many kinds of player, from the most active to the most reflective, and in many styles of piece, from fast show-stopper to slow ballad.

5 *Always leave them wanting more.* There are few things worse than a solo which goes on too long.

6 *Be melodic.* Once you get the facility to be able to play patterns, scales and arpeggios, there is always the temptation to run up and down the instrument rather than improvise a melodic line. Can you sing what you play? Do the phrases breathe? Does it make musical sense?

7 *Go for it!* Never be afraid to take risks or make mistakes. Stretching the boundaries of your playing and of the piece is one of the key ideas of jazz. Safe playing can be boring to listen to.

In your future learning

I hope you have enjoyed learning from this book, and that you will be able to carry away from it not only a range of musical skills but an understanding of how best to learn jazz in the future. Here is a summary of those ideas.

1 *Listen to as much jazz and other music as you can and borrow ideas.* The way to keep moving forwards is to hear music around you all the time and be absorbing it. Music changes around us fast these days, and you can get out of touch very quickly. Borrow ideas you like, transcribe and reuse them.

2 *Don't get stuck in a rut.* There will always be the temptation to use and reuse the same ideas in your playing. If you do this, you will get stale and your playing will lose its freshness.

3 *Rid yourself of habits and clichés.* Listen to your own playing and reassess your vocabulary regularly. Take care not to let technical exercises or patterns become ingrained in your playing, or emerge undiluted by your own ideas in your improvising.

4 *Always make technical practice the starting-point for exploration.* I hope the strategies used in this book have demonstrated ways in which you can integrate improvisation into your scale practice or other technical work. Don't simply play technical exercises for their own sake. Ideally every moment you play the piano should be a musical experience, including scales and aural and quick study work.

5 *Aim for breadth and depth.* Ideally you should be able to play in the widest possible range of styles, and explore the full range of musical possibilities. Don't become too specialized or you will lose work and your musical experience will be less rich. On the other hand, indulge your own obsessions, and really go into depth when you come across a piece of music that is really meaningful to you. If you like it, you will be more motivated to learn from it, and it has probably got something important to say to you.

6 *There is always more to learn.* If you think you know it all, you're wrong! There's always more to discover, and if you are getting stale, move to an environment where the music is more exciting or the teaching is more inspiring or challenging. Avoid complacency at all costs; the humility of all good musicians comes from the realization that the more you know, the more you know there is to learn.

Part III
PREPARING FOR THE EXAM

Good education is not just finding the answers to the questions—it is also questioning the answers.

TREVOR TOMKINS

Chapter 13 # Introduction to the Jazz Piano Syllabus

> Question: Would you regard it as a regression to go back and play your early Sixties compositions?
>
> Wayne Shorter: Not a regression, but it's not what I consider preserving the spirit of jazz. For me, preserving the spirit of jazz means change. That's what jazz is—breakthrough. And for all those young people who want to play like something that was played before, to preserve it, I would say maybe it's better to preserve the process of discovery.
>
> JAZZ JOURNAL, 1996

Part III is focused more specifically on the exams themselves and how to prepare for them. If you've worked through Parts I and II, you should find this preparation straightforward. Before we get onto the detail of the different elements of the exam, here is an overview of the new syllabus—what its aims and key features are and how it differs from previous Associated Board exams.

The vibrant, colourful and highly expressive family of musics that originated in the African American tradition has been part of our lives for a century now. We have all grown up listening to popular music, and we have all been affected by its infectious dancing rhythms, the sense of freedom and spontaneity it engenders and the virtuosity and deep personal commitment of its musicians. Within this family jazz is particularly rich and distinctive. It is more than a hundred years old, but it still has a youthful spirit that searches, changes and grows. It is a music that can be radical and intellectually rigorous, with the highest standards of performing, combining technical accomplishment with great expressiveness.

Why examine jazz?

This music may have been part of our lives, but it has never before been assessed in performing exams at this level. Only in the past twenty years has jazz been formally on music curricula at all, and then often only at university level rather than assessed in its own right in schools. This syllabus aims to change that. A radical departure for the Board, it represents an important shift of direction, a recognition of the importance of jazz and popular music in people's lives, and the huge and previously unrecognized commitment and advanced musical skills of jazz players from Europe, the US and around the world. As anyone who's been teaching jazz in the past twenty-five years will tell you, a progressive, structured and creative set of jazz exams and qualifications has been needed for many years, to give jazz musicians the recognition and credit they deserve.

The preparation of the syllabus has involved several years of careful research by the Jazz Piano Working Party, a forum convened by the Associated Board to set targets and decide the shape of the course. The resulting syllabus is a structure that reflects the experience both of jazz educators and of the Board. The overall shape of the syllabus may be familiar—three lists of pieces, scales, quick studies and aural tests for each grade—but in every detail it has been reconsidered and, if necessary, modified to reflect the requirements of a new idiom.

A new target audience

The new jazz piano syllabus is intended for jazz players of all kinds. But we have specifically tried to include certain kinds of candidate so far excluded from the work of the Board.

First of all, and crucial to the success of the syllabus, we wanted to include the *by ear* candidate, whose knowledge of stave notation might be relatively rudimentary, but who may regularly be playing jazz in clubs and pubs around the country. While the Board feels that the ability to read music is a vital skill, its use in jazz is patchy, and many musicians rightly rely more on their ears than they do on the written note—at its simplest they are able to play jazz skilfully, idiomatically and creatively, but they can't read music.

If such a candidate is able to learn the pieces from the graded CDs and undertake the quick study by ear, the Board has made it possible for them to pass a jazz exam without using stave notation at all. We expect it would be hard for such a candidate to get a Distinction unless they had exceptional aural skills, and by Grade 5 a knowledge of stave notation is highly desirable in order to get through the detail of the increasingly complex pieces, but the fact that the option is there at all is a crucial step forward, and an acknowledgement of the different learning styles that jazz musicians use in approaching their craft.

Secondly we wanted to make the exams open to the *classically trained* candidate, who wishes to expand his or her knowledge and skills into jazz. Jazz originally grew from the complex melting-pot of musics of turn-of-the-century New Orleans, of which classical music, through the French and Spanish influences, was certainly one important element. So there is much in jazz—its harmony, some aspects of the way melody and rhythm work, the whole concept of form and the notation system—that classically trained musicians will find familiar, even though they're often used in very different ways. However, as we stress below, the new syllabus is focused on a different set of skills from that of classical piano. A candidate able to enter Grade 5 classical piano might well have to return to Grade 2 or even Grade 1 jazz piano, in order to get a grounding in the style, the rhythmic language, the improvising and the way in which the written material is treated.

Finally we hope that candidates of all ages and from all ethnic backgrounds will feel they can find worthwhile material to play in the syllabus. Jazz itself is a hybrid music; originating with Africans living in the US, it is now a world phenomenon, featuring internationally renowned soloists from as far apart as Norway (Jan Garbarek), South Africa (Abdullah Ibrahim) and India (Trilok Gurta). If we have got it right, this diversity should be reflected in the pieces, so that players and candidates of all kinds can feel there is something in this syllabus for them.

The new exam

As stated above, the structure of the jazz piano exams is similar to the structure of the current classical piano exams, but the details have been considered afresh according to the needs of the style.

The pieces in the new exam are organized in three lists—Blues, Standards and Contemporary Jazz—and the candidate must play one from each list. The Blues list consists of older and more recent twelve-bar blues tunes by established masters and contemporary composers, and covers the widest possible range of jazz styles and eras in which the twelve-bar blues may be found. The Standards list introduces the candidate to key tunes from the established repertoire, again old and new, in newly written arrangements by contemporary educators and players. And the Contemporary Jazz list is intended as a snapshot of the music of the moment, reflecting the eclectic and sometimes surprising variety of current British jazz. If a candidate learns all the pieces set at each grade, they will have covered a great range of styles.

Compared with the classical piano syllabus, a wider range of species of scale is included, to emphasize the need for flexibility in the candidate's approach to improvising. The scales have also been organized into groups by key, allowing a co-ordinated and progressive approach to learning scales and improvising in the common jazz keys. The aural tests have been newly written for the exam in jazz styles, and at all grades an improvised question and answer test ensures that the candidate can improvise in unprepared contexts and in interaction with the examiner. Finally the quick study also involves improvising, and can be taken by ear or at sight. Further details follow in the relevant chapters.

A new portfolio of skills

A fundamental decision taken early on was *not* just to add new music lists to the existing piano syllabus, but to start from scratch with a wholly new jazz piano syllabus. Although there are clear overlaps between jazz and classical music, there are also many important differences.

Perhaps the most distinctive feature of the jazz piano syllabus is that improvisation is required in every piece from Grade 1, as well as in the aural tests and quick study. The idea of 'performing' a piece in jazz therefore includes not only the ability to *reproduce* accurately given material (heard or from notation), but also the ability to *embellish* given material and to *improvise* or make up new material, to fill a musical space of a particular length and in a particular rhythmic and harmonic context.

The ability to play flexibly and creatively is essential. As with classical music, jazz involves playing fluently, expressively and with control, as well as playing with musical understanding and a sense of style. But in jazz there is a need to *use* that understanding to respond to given chord sequences, rhythmic patterns and other frameworks stylishly, flexibly and creatively on the spot.

Developing a wide and authentic jazz vocabulary and using this in a variety of contexts are also core skills for a jazz musician. Swing, rock and latin grooves, for example, are all part of a basic jazz vocabulary, as is the use of common jazz gestures, rhythmic placements and voicings. Players must be able to cope flexibly with the key features of these styles in all kinds of performing contexts, and have a number of different musical strategies available for coping with particular situations.

Underlying all these skills is the musicianship that makes them possible. Focusing first on rhythm and melody and later, from Grade 4, adding harmony, the whole exam tests the ability of players to think of musical ideas in their head and then to remember and realize them.

Assessment criteria

This new portfolio of skills has led to a new set of assessment criteria. As with the performance skills, these overlap with those of the Board's current classical music syllabuses but differ from them in key respects. A full table setting out the basis of jazz piano assessment is included with the syllabus document; what follows is intended only as an introduction.

Improvisation, which is a key part of the syllabus, is assessed in clearly defined and progressive assessment criteria. For improvisers at Grades 1–3, improvisation is assessed primarily through rhythmic and melodic fluency and basic musicianship skills, with flexibility and musical confidence being the main goals. The emphasis is on getting a flow going, on making good rhythmic and melodic sense using the given guideline pitches, on only playing what you can hear in your head, and on developing the use of other basic musical parameters, such as dynamics, phrasing and playing with character. The ability to make decisions about which pitch goes with which chord is not assessed at these early stages.

At Grades 4 and 5, higher levels of technical control are obviously assumed, as is the beginnings of an understanding of jazz style. This could be demonstrated, for example, in the ability to choose a left-hand part or bass-line appropriate to the style of the given material. A progressively wider range of keys is used in the improvising and scales. In the improvising itself, an ability to choose from a wider range of guideline pitches and whole scales, and to create rhythmic and melodic phrases that are varied, move with and against the rhythmic form of the sequence and use simple motivic techniques is required. The solo sections get progressively longer, until, by Grade 5, there is need to shape them and provide within them a basic variety and contrast to create a sense of rise and fall. From Grade 4, the relationship between melody and harmonic background is assessed, at Distinction level at Grade 4 and at Grade 5 from Pass. In the aural tests, more fluent, varied and confident improvising is assumed, and recognition of elements of the given part is tested.

In jazz there genuinely is more scope for individuality built into the music. Bud Powell, Thelonious Monk, Chick Corea, Erroll Garner and Cecil Taylor are all important jazz pianists and they share a common repertoire, yet their rhythmic sense and their grasp of melody and harmony leads each to quite different and personal sounds, forms and musical gestures. In the same way we have left space in the syllabus for each candidate to make their mark, and to demonstrate that they can find their own way through the tasks shown. If candidates stream in and out of the exam room all sounding identical, we will have failed in possibly the two most important goals of all: first of safeguarding the development of the idiom to which we are so committed, and second of fostering genuine self-expression in a new generation of jazz musicians.

To sum up: the syllabus's major goal is not simply that candidates should be involved in the recreation of set forms of expression. Instead it should empower candidates to discover and develop their own style of playing and improvising through a sound knowledge and understanding of the jazz tradition.

Chapter 14 Pieces

> . . .those moaning saxophones and the rest of their instruments with their broken jerky rhythm make a purely sensual appeal. They call out the low and rowdy instincts . . . Jazz is the very foundation and essence of salacious dancing.
>
> LADIES' HOME JOURNAL, 1921

The pieces in the jazz piano syllabus are divided into three lists: Blues, Standards and Contemporary Jazz. At every grade each list contains five pieces, making a total of 15 pieces in all to choose from. All 15 pieces in each grade are published in a single volume by the Associated Board. You are required to play three pieces in the exam and to choose one piece from each list.

The *Blues list* covers many kinds of blues across the five grades, old and new, from boogie-woogie styles to contemporary compositions, bebop II–V–I blues to modal blues playing. The aim has been to introduce players as far as possible to the widest possible number of variants on the twelve-bar blues form and chord sequence.

The *Standards list* contains core repertoire from the tradition, often in the key in which it is commonly found and in arrangements which duplicate the 'classic' sound of that particular tune. Some have of course been simplified somewhat, but the arrangements have been kept as idiomatic as possible while keeping them accessible and within the tight time constraints of the exams. Some give new slants on familiar compositions.

The *Contemporary Jazz* list contains exclusively new writing, written especially for the syllabus by both established and up and coming jazz pianists and educators, all of whom are working in the field professionally. This list is particularly exciting, contains some excellent new work and represents the Board's commitment to the continuing growth of jazz as an art form that is dynamic, changing and unpredictable.

There is scope for individuality and a degree of creative freedom within the given pieces. They are not arranged chronologically, but if you work methodically through the whole diet given, you should get a solid foundation of knowledge across the full variety of jazz styles possible within the technical limitations of the grade.

The layout of the pieces and the information contained in them has been designed to give candidates as much guidance as possible. Each piece is set out in the same way, as detailed below and as shown in the reprinting of the Grade 1 piece, 'Bottle Junction', by Nikki Iles, printed on page 155. All contain some notated music (the head and possibly a coda) and a section involving improvisation, either a formal solo section or series of improvised breaks, depending on the style of the piece.

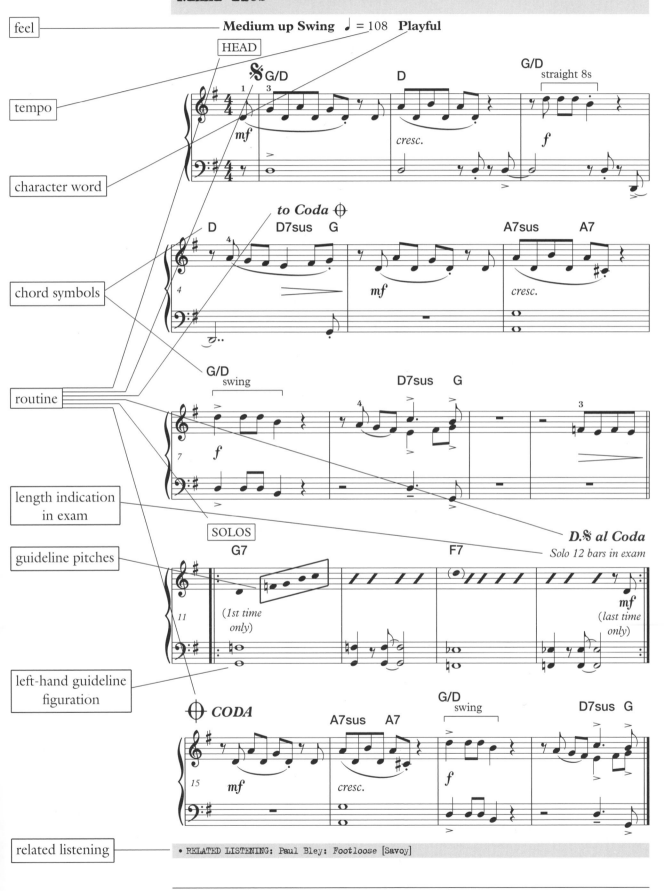

feel

tempo

character word

chord symbols

routine

length indication
in exam

guideline pitches

left-hand guideline
figuration

related listening

BOTTLE JUNCTION
Nikki Iles

Medium up Swing ♩ = 108 **Playful**

HEAD

to Coda ⊕

SOLOS

D.𝄋 al Coda
Solo 12 bars in exam

⊕ *CODA*

• RELATED LISTENING: Paul Bley: *Footloose* [Savoy]

The head

The following specific indications are given in the notated section.

Feel

Each piece is given a feel indication, either swing or straight 8s, and if straight 8s are used, there may be other indications of the exact groove to be followed, for example rock or latin. You should keep to the feel indications in both the notated and the improvised sections.

Tempo

The tempo will be shown as a metronome mark, with either crotchet, quaver or minim = a number, and this should be treated as a *minimum* speed. Check that you have related the metronome marking to the time signature and are not thinking a minim pulse as crotchets, for example!

The tempo marking is an important indication relating to the difficulty level of the piece; if your interpretation falls much below the stated tempo marking you can expect to be marked down, since you will not be able to demonstrate playing at the technical level required for the grade. Ensure you have complete technical control at whatever speed is set, and beware of the danger of missing out details of the pieces given and producing unmusical or unidiomatic results by going much faster than the tempo given.

Character word or phrase

As well as a tempo marking and a feel indication, every piece has been given a character word or phrase by the composer or arranger, which adds colour, gives more information as to the style, mood or character of the piece, and generally helps to define more clearly the kind of interpretation intended. Many of the pieces would otherwise simply be marked 'Medium Swing ♩ = 116' or something similar, and although in jazz that is often all that a player gets in the way of help, learners in the early stages need extra guidance of the kind we have provided.

Routine

Structurally, most but not all of the pieces consist of an opening head, then an improvised section, and then a return to the head or part of the head, sometimes also onto a short coda. Segnos, coda signs and the like have been made *extremely* visible and bold to avoid confusion, but you must work out the routine of the piece carefully and adhere strictly to the given form in the exam. Included in this is an indication at the end of the solos of the exact number of bars or choruses which the solo should last in the exam (see below).

Chord symbols

Simple chord symbols have been given throughout, written above the stave in both head and solos, as would be the case on a chart outside the exam context. In the head they are basically there because they are conventional and because they give a helpful harmonic analysis of the chords used. You might also use them to invent embellishments to the head. In general terms, however, they should be used to facilitate an emerging harmonic understanding of the idiom.

Extensions have been omitted from the given symbols to make them easier to read, though where particularly musically significant, or where the chord sequence makes no sense without them, especially important extensions have been left in to help give sense to the chord sequence given. Candidates will *not* be required to realize extensions in their solos or embellishments up to Grade 5, though those with skills in that area are quite at liberty to use them.

The solos

Chord symbols

In the solos the chord symbols, left-hand guideline figurations and right-hand guideline pitches are included to give full but clear guidance as to how to approach the improvised sections. When learning the piece, stick closely to the given changes, harmonic structures and inner lines stated in the given symbols. In performance, you are not at liberty to introduce *major* modifications of your own to the chord sequence, since part of the challenge is the ability to work within the given harmonic background. However, particularly choice *minor* modifications, substitutions or reharmonizations to individual chords or short progressions of up to two bars in length that occur in the improvisation process are of course idiomatic and to be welcomed, as long as it is clear you know the sequence well in its original form.

It is expected that a gradual progression will occur towards greater flexibility in the treatment of the guideline materials as candidates become more advanced. Specifically they may wish to use the guideline figurations and pitches less and the chord symbols more as a basis for their creative work.

The left-hand guideline figurations

Composers and arrangers have given detailed figurations for use in the left hand in the solo sections for every piece. This is intended to give all candidates an idea of the composer's intentions and the conventions of the style, and gives those less familiar with the style and with good reading skills a leg-up into the process.

They really are *guideline* figurations, however, and it is an important part of the preparation process for the exam that more advanced candidates think of *other* ways of realizing the chords too, based only on the given chord symbols, particularly beyond Grade 3. Outside the exam context, it is normally the case after all for nothing other than chord symbols to be given, and one useful starting-point would be simply to write the chord sequence out as a chord chart and work out a new accompaniment from it. You are expected to extend and develop the given ideas wherever possible to make them your own, and to treat the material as a kind of scaffolding on which to base your own interpretation, rather than a dogma to be followed to the letter in order to pass.

At Grade 1 flexibility in the left-hand work will probably be very limited, and it is entirely acceptable just to play raw semibreves or long notes using the given pitches and concentrate almost exclusively on making effective simple right-hand melodies. By Grade 5, in contrast, those who stick too closely to the given figurations may well not be able to demonstrate the rhythmic flexibility and developmental skills required at the level.

The guideline pitches

The right-hand stave contains one or more groups of guideline pitches (black noteheads without tails) in a rectangular box. These usually coincide with changes in chords, and are positioned accordingly. You should use these as an initial basis for your improvising, though you may of course use others in addition or instead of those given. Once the set of pitches has been given, often taking a bar or half a bar depending on space, the stave is taken up with slashes, indicating further space for improvising using the guideline pitches and others of your choice.

It is generally the case that the guideline pitches given relate directly to the scale syllabus. So if you have learnt the scales for the grade you are taking and the ones before it, you will be prepared for the improvisation associated with that grade. Occasionally, some additional pitches are included, which present good solutions in particular contexts.

As with the left-hand figurations, a gradual increase in flexibility is expected as your skills develop, and the ranges of pitches given reflect this. Choice of pitch is expected also to become more discriminating and distinctive at the higher grades. So at Grade 1, the candidate who uses only the suggested pitches but creates musical and rhythmically inventive phrases will do well; at this level no relationship between melody and harmony is expected. By Grade 5, at the other extreme, more distinctive lines, using a range of intervals and pitches and working over the whole keyboard would be the norm, and melodic lines should bear a clear relationship to any cadential patterns or other harmonic or modal structures given in the chord symbols or left-hand work.

A relationship between melody and harmony is required only in the assessment criteria for Grade 4 (Distinction) and Grade 5 (from Pass), and only these candidates will be penalized for not giving their melodic lines a clear relationship with the harmony. However, you should be learning to work with and across the given harmony *well before this* in your practice, and it is expected that examiners will observe a gradual increase in the relationship between melody and harmony from about Grade 3 onwards.

Length indication and repeat marks

At the end of the solo section each piece contains an indication of the exact length the solo should be in the exam (most often with the exact number of bars). But many of the pieces also contain repeat marks for the solo, to indicate that more repeats are of course possible in performances in other contexts, and to give a form in which the pieces may be played outside the exam. Candidates are strongly encouraged to perform the pieces in a number of different contexts, solo or in a group, playing longer and shorter solos, to practise the flexibility all jazz musicians strive for.

In the exam itself, however, the given solo length indication should be strictly followed. Playing more or less will result in a serious loss of marks and possibly in the examiner stopping you before the end of the piece to keep to time. While this does in a sense go against the free spirit of jazz, it is inevitable to keep the exams running to time, and also gives an added discipline to the process of improvising which is useful in many professional contexts too.

Other information

There are two other items to draw your attention to.

Related listening

At the foot of each piece a CD recording relating to that piece is recommended. In most cases we've given the name of a band or player, an album title (sometimes two) and a specific track name, and the record label. Occasionally we refer more generally to a particular album or to the work of a particular player or band. It is unfortunately the case that many jazz recordings go in and out of print roughly every six months. Every effort was made to ensure that all the CDs listed were available at the time of going to press, but if the one you want has now been deleted, look for a compilation album by the same artist on the same record label, or buy a related album by the same musician or band.

The related listening is intended to encourage study of the playing of the established names in jazz piano and to give an idea in sound of the range of interpretations possible in playing the pieces. In some cases, the track selected may be an interpretation of the tune itself, while in others it may be a track which is related in style, tempo or general character to the piece set. Sometimes the relationship between the given arrangement and the recording is a close one; in others, often the contemporary tunes, the related listening will introduce the broad style rather than the specific piece in question. In any case, even where the related listening is the same tune, it is important to stress that the recording is intended to give ideas, inspiration or a historical context as much as to give you a specific model to work to. Of course, you are not expected to play to the same level of expertise as that of the recording! But at least you'll be able to use some of the ideas you hear as a stimulus for your own playing, and this will encourage you to listen widely and closely to the playing of others.

Notes

A Notes section is given with some pieces. Most often, this relates to the solo, making suggestions for other right-hand pitches to try or ways to vary the left-hand figuration. Occasionally it includes more general information on the piece or refers to specific details in the head.

Preparation

Learning the pieces is perhaps the most demanding part of the process of preparing for the exam, and exactly how to go about it will depend on your aural and notational skills. In each case the aim should be to combine the achievement of technical control and flexibility with a clear and detailed aural image of the piece in your head.

The first two parts of this book are full of guidance on this area. Also, in Chapter 6, we looked in detail at ways to learn the pieces, both from notation and by ear, taking specific pieces from the syllabus by way of example. Follow these suggestions as you learn the pieces for your exam.

In the exam

The examiner will ask you which pieces you are playing. You may play them in any order, and can choose to play them at any point in the exam.

Playing the head

The head of each piece has been carefully composed or arranged and fully notated to include all the characteristic voicings, phrasing and rhythms you need to play the piece with style. For this reason, your starting-point should be to follow the head closely on the first playing. If you're not able to do this, probably you will not do well.

Additionally, a central aim of the jazz piano syllabus is of course to encourage players to respond imaginatively and creatively to the given materials. For this reason, once the playing of the head is firmly under the fingers, you should consider interpreting it more flexibly. You may, for example, introduce variation in details of melody, rhythm, voicing, phrasing, and so on, but the result *must* be coherent, stylish, musical, and not alter the technical level. This is emphatically *not* to allow slipshod playing or an excuse to leave bits out! Ideally, you will be completely comfortable with the given material such that you will be able to play 'beyond' the notes and introduce your own variations. In a nutshell, learn it properly, then play with it.

After the solo(s)

Everything after the solo(s), which is to say the repeat of the head and any coda, may be embellished in a number of ways, from a few simple additions or variations to a more extensive reworking. Exact repetition should be avoided, so as to achieve a more interesting result.

At Grade 1 such embellishment might mean making small melodic or rhythmic changes or varying dynamics or phrasing. At Grade 3 players might change the octaves at which material is played, introduce fills or revoice chords. At Grade 5 harmony may be varied or enriched with extensions, melodic lines may be thickened or ornamented, and rhythms and phrasing reinterpreted. Or none of the above and a completely different set of embellishments! It is for *you* to respond creatively and in your own personal way to the notated material. You have a range of options at all grades and may offer any musical embellishments in keeping with the style.

The graded CDs give examples of the sorts of embellishments you might try, from variations of small details (an additional left-hand kick, a varied right-hand rhythm or grace note) to more extensive reworkings. One piece at each grade has been recorded twice, first minimally embellished, secondly more extensively, in order to demonstrate clearly the range of what is possible. Whatever you do, don't just copy! The examiner will be familiar with the embellishments used on the CD and no credit will be given for slavish copying.

Full details of the assessment criteria for the pieces, showing how marks will be awarded in the different categories and at the various grades, are given in the jazz piano syllabus.

Chapter 15 # The Quick Study

The nature of the music . . . brings to many individuals an unwholesome excitement . . .

LADIES' HOME JOURNAL, 1927

The skills of the quick study could not be more important to the jazz musician. Playing in unfamiliar situations—whether improvising or reading from a chart in a big-band—and with unfamiliar music without sufficient rehearsal, is one of the regular demands placed on a jazz musician; particularly early in their career when they are often a deputy for another player in the band. The ability to keep a cool head in these circumstances and to both recreate and improvise on the spot is a vital survival skill.

So playing unprepared in a lively, creative, musical and accurate way is at the very heart of jazz performance. All jazz musicians have their own vocabulary which they use as a basis for their playing; but they must also be able to improvise unprepared on a piece previously unheard. The quick study tests this ability (without meaning that you should be unprepared for the exam!).

Jazz is an aural tradition, and the ability to pick up new material and recreate it by ear as well as from notation is vital. Some of the most interesting repertoire cannot be written down satisfactorily, and listening and copying is often the only way to get inside the style of the music, its phrasing, its inflections and its expressive embellishments. In order to learn and really understand the style and the repertoire of jazz from the inside, jazz musicians should regularly practise both reading music fluently and musically from the page and copying music fluently and musically directly from what they hear. The Board's quick study, which may be played by ear as well as from notation, provides the building blocks for the development of these necessary skills.

The quick study itself

The quick study consists of two parts: a short head, which should be recreated, followed by a short improvised response. Its layout has been designed to give you as much guidance as possible as detailed below and shown in the reprinting of one of the Grade 1 and Grade 4 practice tests on pp. 164–5.

Feel/groove

The studies cover as wide a range of musical styles within the idiom as possible from the very start. Even at Grade 1, you will need to be able to play in both swing and straight 8 feels, and to use swing, rock and latin grooves. The tempo will also be shown, indicated by a metronome mark, and should be followed.

The scale or mode and guideline pitches

You will be given the scale or mode of the test before playing and, although other pitches may be incorporated as desired, this should form the basis of your improvisation. As in the pieces, guideline pitches are given for those reading from the page, while the name of the relevant scale or mode is given and the initial pitch sounded and named for those working by ear. It is expected that you will be able to use the pitches more flexibly as you progress, working from small three- or four-note pitch groups to full scales as fluency and control develops. As a starting-point you might find it useful to try using the same pitches as those in the short head for your improvisation. Those working from notation may also like to refer to the given chord symbols from Grade 4 onwards, while those working by ear will use the sound of the bass-line as the basis of their harmonic perspective on the given part.

Key signatures

At Grades 1 and 2 the key signature of the quick study follows that of the scale given on which to improvise. At Grades 3 to 5, where the studies are longer, a sense of key or mode emerges. This is reflected in the key signature given.

By ear or from notation

Although it is good practice to work at the tests both ways, it is expected that the majority of candidates will read from notation the given material. However, candidates who play jazz by ear are given the option of reproducing the quick study by ear, after listening to the examiner play the given material. Teachers and students should realize that doing the test this way is not an easy option! The test will be set at a level such that only those with extremely well-developed aural skills and the ability to play by ear efficiently and with great immediacy will be able to do the test in the short time allotted. Ultimately a successful performance of the quick study depends on the musical rendition of the head and a stylish and musical improvisation, not on whether you did it by ear or notation, so you should put your best foot forward in the exam itself.

Preparation

Earlier in this book we discuss at length the virtues in jazz of learning all pieces both by ear and from notation, and those who use these methods will find the quick study integrates well into their normal practice. Working from notation, simply playing through as much material as you can from the start is the best advice, beginning with song sheets or fake books (books of tunes often written simply as melodies with chord symbols). Get used to realizing familiar and unfamiliar melody lines and changes regularly in lessons and private practice time, and then improvising over them.

Working by ear, listen to suitable (and unsuitable!) tapes and CDs, as these will give you ideas for things to reproduce and explore (or avoid!) in lessons. A listening diary may be a starting-point for this, as you can record in it the time you spend listening each week, what to, and perhaps what you particularly liked or which features struck you. Follow this up by detailed study of short extracts from these recordings, learning phrases by singing and playing, and finally turn them into exercises for assimilation and incorporation into your vocabulary. Time spent with a friend or teacher playing question-and-answer games on your instruments is also helpful; begin with one note or a simple, stepwise phrase from an extract at a time, and slowly increase interval range and speed.

For more advanced students, making your own solo transcriptions is a very useful way of improving reading and aural skills as well as increasing vocabulary and knowledge of style. Begin by choosing a recording of a short, perhaps only four-bar, extract from a solo or tune, work it out painstakingly on your instrument by ear from memory and then write it down if this helps you to remember it. Don't forget when studying the music to try and recreate the phrasing, exact timing and dynamics as well as the raw pitches and rhythms—the phrase will only speak if it is played stylishly.

Many notated transcriptions of classic solos by leading players exist, and these can also be used as starting-points, doing the process in reverse, working from notation to real life. Some of these transcriptions are prohibitively hard, however, and the notation is sometimes a hindrance to musical performance, since so much crucial to the style cannot be reproduced. Notation is never useful in jazz without some kind of sound reference. The process of taking something directly from the sound and playing it, without any reference to manuscript paper, fixes the music in the memory in the most thorough way.

Variety in your diet, and little and often are the golden rules, as ever.

In the exam

The quick study for Grades 1 to 5 requires you both to recreate a given short head and also to improvise upon it. At Grades 4 and 5 a simple, repeated left-hand part is included, which continues through both sections. The phrase for recreation will be based on one of the scales included in the technical requirements for each grade or, for Grades 2 and above, from the preceding grades. In the improvising, you should base your response on this scale, which will be indicated. The test may be in either swing or straight quavers, and will indicate whether it is in a swing, rock or latin groove.

If you opt to play at sight, the examiner will give you the pulse and then a short interval of up to half a minute in which to look through and, if you wish, try out any part of the test before you are required to perform it for assessment. The examiner will then count you in.

Here are two examples of the quick study, taken from the book of practice tests. The first example is a Grade 1 test and the second a Grade 4 test.

Grade 1 test

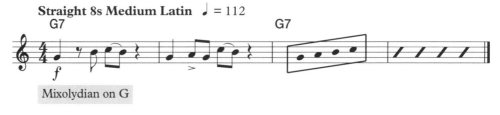

Grade 4 test

Dorian on C

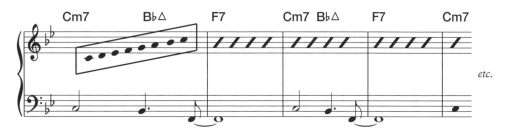

Note the pulse, the tempo and feel indication (given in part by the count-in), the dynamic marking, the key signature, time signature and any other relevant indications. You will be expected to perform the study accurately, fluently and musically from the notation given at the tempo shown. In the improvisatory bars, and in common with the rest of the syllabus materials, guideline pitches, chord symbols and/or a bass-line and the mode or scale are given as appropriate to the level and musical content of the improvisation, and these should be carefully noted too.

If you opt to play by ear, the examiner will state the scale being used, sound and name the starting note or notes, and indicate the pulse. The given passage will be played three times by the examiner, with a short interval after the second and third playings during which you may try out what you've heard and work on your response. Notated music will not be given, and you have to commit to memory the material played by the examiner, including details of its dynamics, phrasing, tempo and groove, as well as work out the basis for the improvisation. For Grades 4 and 5, where the left hand is added, the examiner will play the bass-line as an introductory groove to the first playing (this introduction shouldn't be included in your performance). The examiner will then count you in, clearly indicating the downbeat in cases where the phrase begins after the first beat of the bar.

What the examiner is looking for

The same assessment criteria will apply whether you decide to play the test by ear or from notation (for a complete list of these you should refer to the syllabus). In both cases, credit will be given to those who observe the musical and rhythmic character of the given phrase as well as playing it accurately. If you are working by ear, listen not only to the pitches and rhythms but to the general mood and character, often defined by the speed, the pulse, the rhythmic style, the dynamics and the phrasing. You may find it easier to gain marks by achieving these aspects of the performance, even if the odd pitch is out of place. The examiner will be looking for a sense of performance (keeping going whatever happens) as well as a solid sense of pulse and a positive yet relaxed rhythmic drive.

In the improvised section, you will be expected to make a structured and musical response, in line with the modal indication given. The improvisation should remain broadly within the given style, and should be accurate, technically fluent, inventive and well phrased, although distinctive and lively improvising is also encouraged.

Where inaccuracies occur, credit will be given for a response to the test which puts across the main ideas of the music, the gestures and general character as well as for including as much of the detail as possible. It is better to fumble through the whole thing musically and with great aplomb(!), giving at least a sense of the shape of the whole thing, than to play every note accurately but at a quarter of the real speed with no sense of the music.

Chapter 16   # Scales, Arpeggios and Broken Chords

If Johann Sebastian Bach were alive today, he and Benny Goodman would be the best of friends.

Music Educators' Journal, 1939

The scales and other patterns in the jazz piano syllabus have been organized progressively to develop the technical control, flexibility and knowledge of the geography of the keyboard (i.e. where the sharps and flats are) needed in improvised performance. Crucially, they also relate to the common key centres and roots found in jazz, and introduce patterns characteristic of the style, like pentatonic and blues scales and various modes.

The sense of ease in good jazz playing is usually achieved through regular hard work and the skills developed by the practice of scales and arpeggios. This practice will strengthen your fingers, develop your technical fluency and control, and give you the ability to work accurately both stepwise and across wider leaps.

From the start, practise your scales imaginatively. Save the strict practice and performance of them until close to the exam, and instead be flexible when practising and integrate them with improvisation. The section below on 'creative practice' shows you how.

Patterns

The patterns required for the syllabus are: the major scale, the chromatic scale and the Dorian, Mixolydian and Lydian modes; the blues scale and three forms of pentatonic scale—major, minor and ♭3; and major and minor arpeggios and broken chords built on 7 chords and m7 chords.

The syllabus has been organized to give a range of shapes across each type of scale and pattern through the grades. Systematic and flexible practice of the forms will equip you with the shapes and patterns needed in your playing and improvising.

Key centres and roots

Jazz as an idiom tends to concentrate on fewer keys than classical music, with few sharp keys used beyond A major, because of the preponderance of flat key transposing instruments used. The scale syllabus is therefore organized around fewer key centres and roots, but includes a wider range of patterns in those keys and on those roots. In the early grades the emphasis is on white note roots; thereafter, the progression builds methodically out around the circle of fifths, until by Grade 5 the candidate is able to play several patterns in every key up to three sharps and three flats.

One element this approach gives the improviser is the ability to choose from a number of possible patterns around each *root*. Table 1 lists the patterns by root at the various grades (excluding chromatic scales at Grade 4 (on any black key) and at Grade 5 (on any note)). Notice the initial concentration on the simple white note roots of C, G, D and F, and how by Grade 5 this has extended to roots further afield. Notice also the wide range of patterns on the simple roots learnt by Grades 4 and 5. By Grade 5, for example, a candidate who had worked through the whole syllabus would be able to play all of these patterns on C: the major, blues and chromatic scales; Dorian, Mixolydian and Lydian modes; the three forms of pentatonic scale—major, minor and ♭3; and the minor arpeggio and 7 broken chord. These patterns and shapes make an excellent set of starting-points to use in improvising!

Table 1. Analysis of the scale syllabus by root

Root	Grade 1	Grade 2	Grade 3	Grade 4	Grade 5
C	major major pentatonic	♭3 pentatonic	Mixolydian minor pentatonic blues chromatic minor arpeggio	Dorian C7 broken chord	Lydian
F		major pentatonic	major blues major arpeggio	Mixolydian	Dorian Lydian minor arpeggio F7 broken chord
G	Mixolydian ♭3 pentatonic major arpeggio	major minor arpeggio	Dorian	Lydian major pentatonic G7 broken chord Gm7 broken chord	minor pentatonic blues
B♭			Lydian major arpeggio	major blues	Mixolydian major pentatonic B♭7 broken chord
D	Dorian minor arpeggio	Mixolydian blues chromatic major arpeggio	minor pentatonic	major	Lydian major pentatonic D7 broken chord Dm7 broken chord
E♭				Lydian major pentatonic major arpeggio	major
A		Dorian minor pentatonic	minor arpeggio	Mixolydian major arpeggio Am7 broken chord	major blues
A♭			chromatic		Lydian major arpeggio
E				Dorian minor pentatonic blues	Mixolydian major arpeggio Em7 broken chord
B			chromatic		Dorian minor pentatonic Bm7 broken chord
F♯					blues minor arpeggio

A related but different choice this organization gives to the improviser is the ability to play a number of different patterns in the same *key*. Table 2 provides a similar analysis, this time organized by key centre (again, the chromatic scales are excluded at Grades 4 and 5).

Table 2. Analysis of the scale syllabus by key centre

Key-Centre	Grade 1	Grade 2	Grade 3	Grade 4	Grade 5
C	C major C major pentatonic Mixolydian on G Dorian on D	C♭3 pentatonic A minor pentatonic	C blues chromatic on C C minor arpeggio	G7 broken chord	Lydian on F
F		F major pentatonic	F major F blues F major arpeggio Mixolydian on C Dorian on G Lydian on B♭ D minor pentatonic	C7 broken chord	F minor arpeggio
G	G♭3 pentatonic G major arpeggio	G major G minor arpeggio Mixolydian on D Dorian on A		G major pentatonic Gm7 broken chord E minor pentatonic	G blues Lydian on C D7 broken chord
B♭			B♭ major arpeggio	B♭ major B♭ blues Dorian on C Mixolydian on F Lydian on E♭	B♭ major F7 broken chord G minor pentatonic
D	D minor arpeggio	D blues chromatic on D D major arpeggio		D major Lydian on G Mixolydian on A Dorian on E	D major pentatonic Dm7 broken chord B minor pentatonic
E♭			C minor pentatonic	E♭ major pentatonic E♭ major arpeggio	E♭ major Dorian on F Mixolydian on B♭ Lydian on A♭ B♭7 broken chord
A			A minor arpeggio	A major arpeggio Am7 broken chord	A major A blues Lydian on D Mixolydian on E Dorian on B
A♭			chromatic on A♭		A♭ major arpeggio
E				E blues	E major arpeggio Em7 broken chord
B			chromatic on B		Bm7 broken chord
F♯					F♯ blues F♯ minor arpeggio

Most forms, including the chromatic and blues scales, the ♭3 pentatonic scale and the m7 broken chord, are given under the root from which they begin. The 7 broken chord is treated as chord V, and so C7, for example, is listed under the key centre of F. To demonstrate the progression from key centre to key centre through the grades, the modes have been related to the major key containing the same notes (Dorian on D, Mixolydian on G and Lydian on F therefore appear under C). Remember that every mode can also be used as a scale in its own right, so in modal contexts a piece can actually be in Dorian on D, rather than on chord II of C major. Minor pentatonic scales have been grouped under the key centre of their relative major (thus A minor pentatonic is listed under C).

Notice how scales are grouped so that different keys are emphasized at different grades. A wide variety of forms built around the key centre of F is given at Grade 3, for example; at Grade 5, E♭ and A are more prominent. Once again there is a progression from simpler key centres (C, G and D at Grades 1 and 2) to keys with more sharps and flats at the higher grades. Finally, notice how related major, Dorian, Mixolydian and Lydian patterns are taken as far as possible at the same time or at two consecutive grades. Lydian modes are less common in some styles and therefore occur later in some cases, but by Grade 5 all three modes examined up to and including E♭ and A major are covered.

All of this is balanced by the need also to make the pieces varied and to give the candidate familiarity with as wide a range of roots and key centres as early as possible—if *all* the patterns focused around the same root at each grade, it would clearly give a distorted picture and be rather dull! The emphasis is on building up a range of patterns, starting in simple keys and moving to keys further round the circle of fifths.

Creative Scale Practice

Jazz is all about taking decisions, and being able to realize immediately any music you have decided to play, without fuss and without technical problems impeding the flow. All your work on scales should promote this sense of musical freedom.

With this in mind, practise the patterns as they will actually be used in performance. Simply being able to start and stop on the key-note, for example, is not sufficient—otherwise all improvisations would tend to start and end on this note! You should ideally be able to start and end an improvisation on any degree of the scale, at any speed and at any time, and your practice should lead to this.

In Chapter 7 we looked at some ways to practise scales and integrate them into your improvising. Here now are some further ideas.

Changing Direction

With the forms ascending and descending, practise:

○ beginning and ending on each degree of the scale (using one fingering):

  etc.

○ going back down or up after four, five, six, seven, nine or twelve notes:

  etc.

○ changing direction randomly at a given heard signal from a friend, such as a clap or chord change:

○ changing direction on a downbeat or on an upbeat, or on a given beat of the bar:

  etc.

Rhythm

With and without a metronome, and in both swing and straight 8s, practise:

○ starting on each beat of the bar:

  etc.

○ playing in steady crotchets, quavers, triplet quavers and semiquavers, with and without heavy stresses on the beat;
○ moving from crotchets to quavers every bar, half-bar or beat:

○ starting very slowly and getting steadily faster, or the other way round;
○ moving from straight groove to swung groove on the bar-line;
○ playing with the metronome clicking on beats 2 and 4 of a 4/4 bar, thus simulating a swing groove.

Shape

Practise:
○ scales in steps (as they are normally played);
○ scales in thirds:

 etc.

- scales in fourths:

 etc.

- in groups of three or four:

- inserting extra chromatic notes (for example, B♭ or F♯ in C) so that the line comes out on the beat:

 etc.

- changing from one scale to another in midstream, possibly with additional chromatic notes:

Touch

Practise:
- starting loudly and getting quieter to a soft ending, and vice versa;
- playing *legato* and *staccato*; vary the articulation in different ways within the same scale, for example change every two bars or every beat or offbeat.

The exam

In the exam you need to play the scales and arpeggios from memory. The examiner will normally ask for at least one pattern from each type of scale, arpeggio or broken chord required at that grade, and from Grade 1 can ask for the patterns to be played in swing or straight 8s.

Examiners will be looking for the following qualities in your playing of the technical requirements:

- accurate and fluent realization from memory of the patterns set for the grade
- even tone across all five fingers of both hands
- independence of the fingers
- an even and positive sense of pulse and rhythm
- a knowledge of the geography of the keyboard
- smooth negotiation of common technical problems, for example, putting the thumb underneath, dealing with awkward leaps, running out of fingers, etc.

The book of *Jazz Piano Scales* sets out all the requirements by grade and provides fingerings for each, sometimes with alternatives. The short introduction also includes a table of recommended minimum speeds for the various patterns at the five grades.

Chapter 17   # Aural Tests

> **Though it may shock the idolators of the masters, it is fair to say that Ellington is a composer in the tradition of Bach and Haydn.**
>
> NEW YORK TIMES, 1940

Aural and musicianship skills are a fundamental part of jazz performance and improvisation. In solo work jazz musicians must hear in their head the rhythmic and harmonic context in which they are working, in order to respond inventively and stylistically to that sound in their improvisation. In ensemble playing musicians must make choices about their role within the overall texture and the notes or rhythms that are most appropriate to play in the light of what they hear. The Board's aural tests are designed to help you to listen to music in this way and to foster working by ear, the best and often the only way to learn jazz.

Jazz musicians use their aural and analytical skills to fix a clear and detailed 'inner aural image', or 'internal map', of a piece of music in their heads. This map will provide the structure—important rhythmic, melodic, harmonic and formal features—upon which any successful improvisation will be made. When you are improvising over chord sequences, having a good inner map is doubly important because you may have to use that map to cut your *own* route through the jungle, and not just depend on the roads others have already ridden. Simply learning patterns—'Left at the 7th chord, second right at the syncopated accent and keep going until you get to the final cadence'—will not be enough. The player must know *several* ways of getting from the beginning of a tune to the end and get an idea of the whole terrain: perhaps preparing a really off-the-wall route involving interesting back alleys; a route that involves green fields and stopping to smell the flowers, or a hell-for-leather motorway route with high-speed chases!

So jazz musicians need a detailed composer's eye view of the music. The aural image must be complete, cover all the main concepts used in the piece, and be so well ingrained that the musicians have an *intuitive* sense of direction and can explore without getting lost and without continually having to check where they are on the map. All of this involves many generally important aural skills, which include:

1   The ability to remember sounds. Develop a good memory, trained week by week, until things really stick.
2   The ability to understand and use fundamental concepts. What exactly is a rhythm, a pulse, a melody, a 7th chord, a twelve-bar chorus, a rock groove? How do they fit together to build up a complete picture?
3   The ability to recognize, copy and use commonly recurring patterns and features, such as chords, intervals, rhythms, forms, etc.
4   The ability to recreate and use those sounds in singing and playing.

Several other guiding principles lie behind the design of the aural tests for the jazz piano syllabus. First and most importantly they are designed to give the improviser skills as relevant to their practice as performers as possible. Secondly all the tests are designed to integrate, as far as possible, with the practice of learning how to play jazz, rather than be some kind of special imposition only to be added to the candidate's experience as part of an assessment process. Question and answer clapping, and later singing, both using echoes and inventing responses, is an excellent way of warming up at the start of any lesson and can be developed, as we have seen, directly into improvising on an instrument. New feels, styles, time signatures and other rhythmic and melodic vocabulary may be introduced through these exercises, and the ones in the tests focus the mind on the all-important rhythmic elements of the music right from the start.

If you have been using the ideas and methods suggested throughout this book, you should find yourself well prepared for the aural tests. Questions along the lines of 'What feel is this in?', 'How many beats in a bar are there?', 'How does this rhythm go?' and 'Can you clap the pulse?' are almost bound to occur in the course of learning pieces and developing improvisation skills. Specific preparation for the aural tests should therefore normally only involve reducing nerves by getting comfortably familiar with the format of the test. As the exam approaches, regular practice runs should be undertaken, in which questions are asked in the order used in the exam and with the time allowed for answering the questions, and number of repetitions of the question given, being roughly the same as would be expected under exam conditions.

There follows a test-by-test breakdown, with a description of each test, and advice on attempting it. Each is divided into sections as follows: 1) Preparation, 2) Taking the test, and 3) What the examiner is looking for. Ensure that you have also read carefully the exam rubric contained in the syllabus itself, however, as what follows assumes a knowledge of the tests themselves, and is *not* in itself part of the syllabus.

Test A

This test consists of several elements, organized around a single piece of music heard, as follows:

A1: Clapping the pulse (Grades 1–3), or stating the time and groove (Grades 4–5)

Preparation

A1 practises your ability to count along with a given extract—if you like, to play along in your head. Hearing a pulse is easier than reproducing it, particularly for beginners. Sometimes hand-clapping does not work first time, so try foot-tapping or counting beats of the bar out loud. You can practise doing this exercise on any other material you are working on or like. 'What time is this in?' is always a good first question to ask yourself when starting on a piece, and should always be followed up by practical tapping or clapping as well as looking at the time signature. This will ensure that you are not simply reading or guessing but actually understand and can hear what a bar of that length sounds like. Supplement this by using tapes and music in the widest possible variety of styles: swing and straight 8 feels, rock, latin and swing grooves, at a variety of tempos and in all relevant times, including 2, 3, 4 and 5 as appropriate to the level. Include some classical music too.

Working out the number of beats in a bar is related directly to finding the first beat. Try and work out the answer for yourself by listening. Crucial questions are, 'How do you know where the down beat is?' and 'How often does it come?'. The placement exercises in Chapters 1 and 7 will help here. Remember that while the first beat may be stressed, swing and rock grooves also have regular and irregular stresses on other beats too, often two and four, so looking for regular sequences of stresses will help.

At Grades 4 and 5 you will need to state the groove of the extract as well as the time. The differentiation of swing from rock and latin is relatively easy, because of the swing feel. Both rock and latin grooves are broadly in simple time in straight 8s, however, and differentiation of these two grooves often relates to stresses in the rhythmic structure, which may be expressed in the bass-line. A regular offbeat stress in the bass-line, particularly on the 'and of 2' (fourth quaver in a 4/4 bar) is a common feature of latin music, as is the anticipation of beats across the barline (beat 1, for example, may appear as the 'and of 4'). Rhythmic interplay between left and right hands and between bass-line, chordal accompaniment and melody is also common.

Rock grooves are more solidly on the beat, with repeating rolling quaver and crotchet rhythms, and sometimes have more solid chordal textures. In general, rock piano touch tends to be heavier. Listen to recordings of as wide a range of music in these styles as possible. You will find that playing notated pieces in these grooves will also help.

Notice that both swing and straight feels and swing, rock and latin grooves are used from the start, so these fundamental ideas must be in place from Grade 1.

Taking the test

At Grades 1 to 3 the examiner will ask you to clap the pulse of a piece of music, and you should join in as soon as you've got it. At Grades 4 and 5, you will instead be asked to state the time and groove of a piece played, and this will be a simple and clear matter of choosing between the available options at the level (2, 3 and 4 at Grade 4; 2, 3, 4 and 5 at Grade 5; swing, rock or latin). Note that a '2' feel is likely to be a 2/2 feel—a half time samba or swing feel—rather than 2/4.

What the examiner is looking for

1 Confident, prompt and accurate response
2 Grades 4–5: accuracy in identifying time—2, 3, 4 or 5 depending on level
3 Grades 4–5: accuracy in identifying the groove—answers should be confined to stating 'swing', 'rock' or 'latin' as appropriate

A2: Clapping on a specified beat or sub-beat of the bar

This second part of the test is designed to develop the important jazz skill of rhythmic flexibility, whereby a player is able to place a note or chord, or begin a musical phrase, at any point desired in the bar.

A common problem with those beginning to improvise is a lack of rhythmic variety. One symptom of this is when students consistently start their improvised phrases at the same point in the bar. Some always start on the first beat, for example, while others will wait and begin somewhere on beats two or three. In practising this test you will develop the ability to choose where in the bar to begin and end a phrase and will acquire the technical confidence to do so.

Preparation

You will find some beats easier to clap on than others, and should work particularly to improve those areas where there is weakness. The easiest way to improve is systematically to work through the beats of the bar, one by one. The sections on rhythmic placement in Chapters 1 and 7 provide many useful activities which will help you to do this.

Taking the test

The examiner will tell you on which beat, or sub-beat for Grades 4 and 5, you should clap and will then count in and play the extract a second time. You will be expected to come in clearly and confidently from the first bar.

What the examiner is looking for

1 Immediate response
2 Accurate, confident and relaxed articulation of the beat required
3 For Grades 4 and 5, where sub-beats are required, that the feel (swing or straight) is reflected in the sub-beat clapped

A3: Clapping the rhythm of a short extract

Preparation

Hearing a rhythm and copying it *exactly* is the skill here. No improvisation is required and would be a positive hindrance! Listen carefully to the very end of the phrase, as well as to the start, and copy accurately. In many of the tests, simple rhythmic ideas recur several times, so it is worth working on identifying short rhythmic motives that repeat within longer phrases. Time spent learning to recognize common chunks of rhythmic vocabulary from recordings or live performances will also help with this test, as the same kinds of phrases will inevitably tend to recur in the style.

Listen regularly to phrases and clap them, from the music you are learning to play, from examples you make up and from recordings or transcriptions of established players. Listening and copying is in fact the best way to learn new vocabulary for your improvisations, so if you are spending time listening to musicians you like and copying their playing, again you should be well prepared.

Another important stage in the process is learning to hold a rhythm in your head for a while before clapping it back. Practise this by getting your teacher or a friend to clap you a rhythm and then think it through *in your head* only, before attempting to clap it back. You can even try inserting a 30-second pause between hearing the rhythm and clapping it back, in which you clap it back to yourself several times before actually completing the test. When you are practising, ask for as many repetitions of the rhythm as you need, and don't clap it back until you're absolutely certain you have it in your head accurately. It is even worth saying out loud in practice sessions what you do and don't remember: 'I've got the first half, but there's still a small bit in the second half I've not quite got clear in my mind', so that you consciously go through this process of assessment.

Taking the test

The examiner will play the set rhythm extract (taken from the A test and bracketed clearly in the specimen book) twice. You will only hear the part of the piece containing the rhythm and not the whole texture of the bracketed section. Listen carefully to the phrase and clap the phrase straight back after the final time, having used the gap between the hearings to play it back to yourself. Unless you are *extremely* confident, resist the temptation to have a go before hearing the extract for the second time, as you will lose marks if you get it wrong.

What the examiner is looking for

1 A steady pulse
2 Accurate reproduction of the phrase given, including accents and other phrasing where appropriate
3 The ability to keep going if you make a mistake

Test B

Singing as an echo (Grades 1–3)

This test, which follows on naturally from the copying of a rhythm, emphasizes the need for singing and memory work to be a central part of learning to improvise, helping in the development of both internal and external pitching.

Preparation

This particular test requires the ability to feel a regular length of bar or phrase and the ability to come in on the beat of the bar given, as well as a good memory. Build on the clapping rhythm games you have already been working on by introducing pitch-copying as a new element. Initially use the voice, but later you can also practise at the keyboard. Use one, two or a maximum of three pitches in very focused copying work to begin with. Try adding some chordal accompaniment, perhaps a simple groove from one of the pieces, to fill out the texture if you want. As the grades progress, the pitch range used gets wider, so it is worth gradually introducing new and named intervals—a perfect fourth, then a fifth, then a sixth and so on—into your practice. This will lay the foundation for the test involving interval recognition at Grades 4 and 5.

As you progress, copying games can be done with both singing and playing. Work towards a format where you have to play then sing, and also sing then play, the same phrase. This will take patience at the start but pays dividends in the long run, eventually leading to integration of ear, voice and hand. Some improvisers sing what they play at the same time in performance—George Benson and Keith Jarrett are two examples.

You may be able to sing well but find playing harder, or play well but find it harder to sing. Try working by singing and playing at the same time, to link the hand and the voice.

Taking the test

The examiner will count in the test and then play four two-bar phrases one after the other. There will be a space between each for you to sing the copied answer. The pulse will continue evenly and without stopping once it has begun, so your echo must follow each phrase in time and without a pause: this is intentionally a quick-fire test with no time to hesitate and requires quick musical reactions. Unlike the rhythm test, the crucial thing here is to have a go at each phrase straightaway, and not to wait until you feel ready. Listen carefully to the two-bar count-in which will set up a solid pulse and give you a sense of the structure of the whole test, as well as remind you how many beats in a bar there are.

What the examiner is looking for

1 Accurate placement of the beginning of each phrase
2 Accurate reproduction of the phrase given
3 The ability to keep going undeterred if one phrase is missed

Remember that beautiful tone is less important than accuracy!

Test C (Grades 1–3), Test B1 (Grades 4–5)

Question and answer/improvised answering phrases

This test practises the invaluable technique of question and answer—a technique used by improvisers and composers in jazz all the time. They will invent melodies containing answering phrases, play 'fours', where one musician plays a question and another responds to it, and sometimes improvise and compose riffs or vamps which work in question and answer textures. In this text you will be required to reproduce something of the style of the given phrase and to create a simple yet effective improvisation, and this may be done with the voice or at the piano.

Preparation

Concentrate first on the pitches of the given phrase; initially simply copy the given phrase and perhaps alter one note. Later, confidence will lead to greater freedom.

In the improvisations use sequences or motivic repetition and development wherever possible; use spaces to create interesting phrase lengths; contrast dynamics, or introduce some kind of distinctiveness, such as an accent, a surprise, an anticipation, a gap or contrast of fast with slow singing.

There are many activities in this book to develop question-and-answer techniques. Look back at Workshop 6 in Chapter 1 (p. 14) for rhythm games and the activities introducing pitch in Chapter 2 (p. 19).

Taking the test

The examiner will count in the test, set up the groove for four bars and then play four two-bar melodic phrases (with accompaniment), with gaps for improvised answers between each. There will be no pause between each, and the pulse will continue evenly and without stopping once it has begun. As with the echo test, the skill here is quick-fire musicianship; the ability to respond immediately, intuitively and without too much conscious thought to a given musical stimulus.

What the examiner is looking for

1 A flexible and creative response to the question
2 Evidence that the candidate has identified the given rhythmic style and tempo, and can work within it
3 Musical (though not necessarily predictable) rhythmic phrasing
4 Improvised answers containing commonly used jazz devices which may include any of the following:

   ○ the reproduction of elements of the question (without copying it entirely!)

   ○ devices for creating rhythmic interest, such as leaving gaps, use of surprise, polyrhythm, and varying stressed and unstressed notes

Test B2 (Grades 4–5): Recognizing intervals

As we have seen earlier in the book, the recognition of intervals is the key to an aural understanding of harmony and melody.

Preparation

The main guideline here is to ensure that the first time you meet an interval is not the first time you try to do these aural tests. The interval concept should be well embedded in your experience before an exam is attempted.

The start of Chapter 8 goes through all the types of interval and shows you how to integrate interval study into your improvising. Go through these various activities to make sure you know and can recognize the different intervals.

Taking the test

The examiner will play two melodic intervals taken from the four two-bar phrases just heard. In each case you will hear the interval twice, note by note and at a register suitable for your voice, and you should then sing back the two pitches in order and give the interval's name. At Grade 4 the intervals will range from a major 2nd to a perfect 5th and at Grade 5 from a minor 2nd to a major 6th (both grades exclude the tritone).

What the examiner is looking for

1 Accurate pitching of the two notes played
2 Correct identification of the interval, e.g. major sixth

Vamps and Bass-lines

Here are some of the most common vamps and bass-lines, to be used as starting-points for exploration and practice. All are very common jazz piano clichés, used widely as accompaniment textures—invent your own variations as you like. They are arranged broadly by style but many can be played in both swing and straight 8s contexts and at a number of speeds.

First learn them by heart in *both* keys. Play them as repeating patterns and then improvise over or around them as you feel, taking elements relevant to any pieces you are working on. Then use the patterns in chord sequences, transposing the given lines and voicings to suit the chords of the piece you are working on. Some are easier than others, so simply choose one that suits your own technical level, ensuring that you can play it with sufficient ease to improvise in the right hand too. Enjoy!

Blues

(Swing or Straight 8s)

Standards

(Swing)

Contemporary Jazz

Rock

(Straight 8s)

Jazz Waltz

(Swing)

Rock Ballad

Latin

(Straight 8s)

Listening Guide

Here is a list of key albums which you should find and listen to. You'll notice that many are ensembles containing pianists: most jazz piano takes place in a group context and much of the best jazz piano playing has been done in small groups where the pianist was not the feature. We've aimed to provide a full range of piano styles and most of the main names are represented.

Artist or group	Album	Pianist
Miles Davis	Round Midnight	Red Garland
	Kind of Blue	Wynton Kelly / Bill Evans
	Milestones	Red Garland
	My Funny Valentine	Herbie Hancock
Stan Getz	Anniversary	Kenny Barron
Modern Jazz Quartet	Blues at Carnegie Hall	John Lewis
Sonny Rollins	Saxophone Collosus	Tommy Flanagan
Cannonball Adderley	At the Lighthouse	Victor Feldman
	Somethin' Else!	Hank Jones
Bill Evans Trio	Sunday Night at the Village Vanguard	Bill Evans
Art Blakey's Jazz Messengers	Ugetsu	Cedar Walton
	At Birdland (with Clifford Brown)	Horace Silver
John Coltrane Quartet	Coltrane (Impulse)	McCoy Tyner
Charlie Parker—Dizzy Gillespie	Jazz at Massey Hall	Bud Powell
Keith Jarrett Trio	Standards Volume II	Keith Jarrett
Ben Webster	Ben Webster Meets Oscar Peterson	Oscar Peterson
Bill Evans—Toots Thielmans	Affinity	Bill Evans
Chick Corea	Three Quartets	Chick Corea
Herbie Hancock	Maiden Voyage	Herbie Hancock
	Headhunters	
Weather Report	8:30	Joe Zawinul
Charlie Mingus	Mingus Ah Um	Horace Parlan
Wes Montgomery	The Incredible Jazz Guitar	Tommy Flanagan

Artist or group	Album	Pianist
Big Bands		
Duke Ellington	At Newport	Duke Ellington
Count Basie	The Complete Atomic Mr Basie	Count Basie
Woody Herman	Encore	
Miles Davis / Gil Evans	Miles Ahead	Gil Evans
Mel Lewis—Bob Brookmeyer	At the Village Vanguard	
Recent Developments		
Abdullah Ibrahim	African Horns (1989)	Abdullah Ibrahim (Dollar Brand)
Bheki Mseleku	Celebration (1992)	Bheki Mseleku
Julian Joseph	Reality (1993)	Julian Joseph
Perfect Houseplants	Clec (1995)	Huw Warren
Michel Petrucciani	Both Worlds (1997)	Michel Petrucciani
Julian Arguelles Octet	Skull View (1997)	Mario Laginha

(Compiled by Trevor Tomkins and used with permission.)

Glossary

anticipation   anticipating a beat by playing a note or chord on the previous quaver or crotchet

augmentation   process in which the rhythmic values of notes in a phrase are doubled

augmented   altering an interval by raising it a semitone; most commonly, the augmented 4th, e.g. C–F♯

backbeat   the stress on beats 2 and 4 in jazz and rock grooves

beat   refers to a given place in the bar, e.g. beat 1, beat 2, etc. Also used in the context 'got a good beat' to refer generally to the style, driving quality and success of a given groove.

bebop   challenging, complex and exciting virtuoso jazz style of the 1940s. Charlie Parker (alto sax), Dizzy Gillespie (trumpet), Thelonious Monk (piano) and Bud Powell (piano) are key names.

boogie-woogie   early 1900s piano style, combining a driving 'train-style' left hand with characteristics of the blues. Key players include Clarence Pinetop Smith, Meade Lux Lewis and Pete Johnson.

bossa nova   popular early 1960s latin jazz style blending Brazilian rhythms and grooves with cool jazz. Key players include Joao Gilberto, Stan Getz, Charlie Byrd and Oscar Peterson. Key composer: Antonio Carlos Jobim.

break   short melodic phrase which punctuates the music, usually while the accompaniment stops

bridge   name for the contrasted B section of a 32-bar standard (AABA), also called the middle eight. May occur in other tunes with contrasting middle sections.

calypso   style of music, dance and song originating in the West Indies, popularized in the 1930s and 1940s, and taken up by jazz musicians including Sonny Rollins, Nat 'King' Cole and Dizzy Gillespie. Sometimes characterized by regular accents on beat 1 and the 'and' of 2.

changes   name given to the string of chords used in a piece or section of it; 'Rhythm Changes' describes the sequence of chords from the bridge of Gershwin's 'I Got Rhythm', used in many standards

chord   sound formed by two or more notes played together

chord sequence   led from the bass-line, a series of chords in a repeating sequence that make up the harmonic background to a tune or solo section

chord symbol   concise designation of the notes of a chord placed above the stave (sometimes between the staves), consisting of the root note and a symbol indicating the remaining possible notes, e.g. CΔ = a major 7 chord on C, i.e. the notes C E G B. Some chords may be referred to by more than one symbol, e.g. Cmaj7 = CΔ; D– = Dm. See also triad over bass note.

clave   set of stresses across a 4/4 bar in latin grooves; pronounced 'clah-vay'

closed position   type of voicing in which the notes of the chord are close together

comping   short for 'accompaniment'. Creation of a rhythmic and harmonic background for your own melodies or for other players' solos.

consonant   description of an interval, chord or general character of a piece or section where the sound is smooth and rounded

degree   name for the pitch of a scale, defined by its position from the root; e.g. the 3rd degree of C major is the note E

diminished   altering an interval by lowering it a semitone; most commonly, the diminished 5th, e.g. D–A♭

diminution   process in which the rhythmic values of notes in a phrase are halved

dissonant   description of an interval, chord or general character of a piece or section where the sound is harsh or discordant

Dixieland jazz   see New Orleans jazz

downbeat the downbeats are beats 1, 2, 3 and 4, while the upbeats are the 'ands' of each of these beats, that is to say the 'offbeat' quavers, in classical terms. Originally called down and up because of the relationship with dance and the position of the body as down or up.

extensions notes added to a chord for extra dissonance and richness; named using numbers above 8, most frequently the 9th, 11th and 13th. May sometimes be sharpened or flattened.

feel the way the beat is subdivided. Subdivision into 2 is known as straight 8s; subdivision into 3 as swing.

free jazz The avant-garde jazz of the late 1950s and 1960s, characterized by experiments with atonal and other harmony, using more than one pulse or none at all and a general concern with extremes and breaking the boundaries of jazz. Key players include Ornette Coleman, late John Coltrane and Cecil Taylor.

funky funk was a style of mid-1960s and later American popular music which developed from Motown and Soul, often characterized by repeating semiquaver syncopations around a 4/4 rock groove

groove name given to the rhythmic character of a piece of music; defined by its bass-line, pattern of accents and offbeats and style. Broad categories are swing, latin and rock. In jazz, grooves may be varied, particularly in solo sections.

guide tones notes of a chord, typically the 3rd and 7th, which 'guide' the harmony by the way they move, creating and releasing harmonic tension

hammering on blues technique describing the addition of a repeated note above a melody, 'hammering' with it in the same rhythm

head jazz musician's term for the tune, the often written-out music that comes at the beginning or 'top'. A common signal at the end of an improvisation is for the leader to point to his or her head, which means 'Back to the top, let's play the tune again, I'm finishing my solo.'

inner lines contrapuntal lines linking the guide tones in chordal progressions

internal clock a clear sense of the pulse which you feel within yourself

interval the gap between two notes, e.g. minor 3rd, major 7th. Can describe notes played melodically or harmonically.

inversion description of chords, dependent on their bass note. A C major chord with C in the bass is in root position; with E as the lowest note it's in first inversion, and with G in the bass it's in second inversion.

jazz-rock late 1960s and early 1970s style, incorporating jazz improvisation with rock grooves and often electric instruments. Sometimes known as 'fusion'. Key players include Miles Davis (*Bitches Brew*), Herbie Hancock (*Headhunters*), the band Weather Report (*Heavy Weather*) and the band Blood, Sweat and Tears.

jazz waltz 3/4 swing groove, often using the characteristic hi-hat pattern

and sometimes a stress on the 'and' of beat 2. Used frequently by pianist Bill Evans, e.g. the tunes 'Alice in Wonderland' and 'Some day my Prince will come'.

key description of a piece or section of a piece in which the music adheres in general (there may be a number of chromatic notes) to the notes of a major or minor scale. A piece 'in the key of' C major, e.g., will contain a melody using principally the notes of this major scale and chords derived from it.

kicks points of rhythmic emphasis in a given melody, often stressed by the accompanying left hand or bass and drums

latin global term encompassing a number of rhythmic styles within jazz, combining improvisation with the rhythms of Latin America, including bossa nova, samba or salsa

lick short melodic or rhythmic phrase that becomes characteristic of a player's or group's style

major description of intervals (not 4ths, 5ths or octaves) where the gap between the two notes is the greater possible alternative: e.g. C to E in a major 3rd (cf. C–E♭, a minor 3rd). Description of a chord where the 3rd is major and of a scale where the succession of intervals is tone, tone, semitone, tone, tone, tone, semitone.

medium swing   see swing (1)

middle eight   see bridge

minor   description of intervals (not 4ths, 5ths or octaves) where the gap between the two notes is the smaller possible alternative: e.g. C–E♭ in a minor 3rd (cf. C–E, a major 3rd). Description of a chord where the 3rd is minor and of two possible types of scale where the succession of intervals at the top varies but where in each case the 3rd is a minor 3rd.

mode   type of scale with a distinct arrangement of tones and semitones. Examples are the Dorian, Mixolydian and Lydian modes.

modulation   the movement within a piece or section of a piece from one key to another

motive   short musical idea—rhythmic, melodic or harmonic—used as the basis for development in improvisation

neighbour notes   notes a step away from the note concerned in the scale. Chromatic notes are notes a semitone away.

New Orleans jazz   early style of small-ensemble jazz originating in New Orleans in the 1910s and 1920s, from which many later styles, revivals and imitations (Dixieland, Traditional) emerged

open position   type of voicing in which the notes of the chord are spaced for clarity

perfect   description of the intervals of a 4th and 5th in their usual position: e.g. C–F (4th), C–G (5th)

polyrhythm   superimposition of one rhythm or pulse upon another

pulse   created by the division of time into regular beats at a particular speed

Rhythm and Blues   (R'n'B)   guitar-based blues style that grew up alongside jazz, continued the boogie-woogie tradition within jazz piano and led, in one offshoot, to rock-n-roll in the 1950s

rhythm section   usually the piano, bass and drums, sometimes also with guitar and percussion. A group of instruments whose role is to define the groove and then vary it continually throughout a solo, creating a range of textures and dynamics in interaction with the soloist. They also provide a rhythmic and harmonic context for a solo and sometimes take on a more soloistic role themselves. In more popular styles the rhythm section tend to be more fixed in their roles, while in jazz they are given more flexibility.

rhythmic placement   the ability to place a note, phrase or chord on a particular place in the bar

riff   a repeated melodic phrase or bass-line. Often used in interaction with a given texture or with other riffs to create an exciting polyphonic texture or build-up behind a solo or melody.

rock   (1) led from the bass-drum, a rock groove is usually in 4/4 and has a backbeat on beats 2 and 4, often on the snare drum in a band context (2) global term for a number of styles of guitar-based popular music, which grew from rock-n-roll and first became popular in the 1950s and 1960s

root   the bass note of a chord

samba   latin 2 feel groove, with an accent on beat 2. Felt at a walking pace, it was originally the music of carnival, but is now found at a range of tempos.

Scat singing   vocal improvising, usually without words, or where words are made up that create good textures or appropriate attacks for the rhythmic character of the improvising

sequence   see chord sequence

seventh chord   chord formed from the root, 3rd, 5th and 7th degrees of a scale. Often voiced with 5th omitted.

slow swing   see swing (1)

song form   name given to the structure of a typical 32-bar standard: AABA. The B section is known as the middle eight or bridge.

straight ahead jazz   sometimes also called mainstream. Grew out of bebop and the various jazz movements of the 1950s, and implies the conventional or straightforward jazz of bebop and its derivatives. Usually swing feel, and contrasted with the more eclectic approaches of latin jazz, jazz-rock and free jazz.

straight 8s   feel indication in which the beat is subdivided into two

stride   style of jazz piano playing in which the left hand 'strides' between bass notes or (rolled) 10ths on beats 1 and 3 of a 4/4 bar and chords around the middle of the keyboard on beats 2 and 4. Notable exponents were 'Fats' Waller and Art Tatum.

substitution   replacement of one or more chords of the standard blues sequence with others, to create a richer effect or provide more movement

swing   (1) led from the ride cymbal, swing is a feel indication in which each beat is subdivided broadly into three —a triplet feel. Often seen at the start of a melody as slow swing, medium swing or up swing, indicating the tempo concerned. Common in jazz from the 1920s to the present. (2) style of jazz that also became the popular music of the 1930s and 1940s, characterized by the big band sound and the triplet subdivision (see (1) above). Key players included Count Basie, Duke Ellington and on piano 'Fats' Waller, Art Tatum and Erroll Garner. Also, in the more commercial form, Benny Goodman, Tommy Dorsey and Glenn Miller.

syncopation   stressing notes other than the main beats of the bar

tendency tones   another name for guide tones

ten-to-ten   name for the characteristic swing rhythm played on the ride cymbal of a drum-kit. In 4/4 it is heard as:

Traditional jazz   see New Orleans jazz

triad   chord formed from the root, 3rd and 5th degrees of a scale

triad over bass note   style of harmony, where chords are created by choosing a bass note and a triad to go above it, which creates a particular modal context for improvising. Used particularly after 1950 as a way of widening the available palette of chords and voicings. Also a way of notating these chords, e.g. B♭/C = a triad of B♭ over a C bass note. (see also chord symbol)

triad tones   tones 1, 3 and 5 of a given triad, often used to create the backbone of an improvisation over that triad

turnaround   chordal progression at the end of a section or solo and leading to the next section or back to the head. (I)–VI–II–V is a typical example.

twelve-bar blues   chord sequence lasting twelve bars which became popular and standardized in the early part of the century and has formed the basis of much popular music and jazz since then. Also implies a particular melodic vocabulary and a way of playing.

II–V–I   'two-five-one'; name of a common chord progression using the chords IIm7–V7–IΔ

upbeat   see downbeat

up swing   see swing (1)

vamp   repeated phrase, often containing a particular rhythmic, melodic and harmonic character or idea; useful to improvise over and often found in the introductions to tunes or as a holding device at particular points in jazz forms

voicings   The spacing, layout and combination of notes in a chord which helps produce the characteristic sonorities within different jazz styles

walking bass   often on the (plucked) string bass, a steady crotchet line at the bottom of a swing texture which defines a swing groove and creates the harmonic basis by stating and interacting with the roots, triad tones and other notes in the harmony

List of Quotations

Introduction
Wynton Marsalis: 'Why we must preserve our jazz heritage', *Ebony*, February 1986, pp. 131 ff.
Eddie Harvey: jazz educator.

Part I
Susan Jeffers: *Feel the Fear and do it Anyway* London, republ. 1997

Chapter 1
Trevor Tomkins: drummer and jazz educator.

Chapter 2
Gary Bartz: in Paul Berliner, *Thinking in Jazz: The Infinite Art of Improvisation* (Chicago, 1994), p. 247.

Chapter 3
Billie Holiday: on her time with the Basie Big Band, in Paul Berliner, *Thinking in Jazz: The Infinite Art of Improvisation* (Chicago, 1994), p. 305.

Chapter 4
Keith Jarrett: quoted in Ian Carr, *Keith Jarrett: The Man and his Music* (London, 1991), p. 59.

Chapter 5
Eddie Harvey: jazz educator.

Chapter 6
Edward A. Berlin: quoted in Kathy Ogren, *The Jazz Revolution: Twenties America and the Meaning of Jazz* (New York, 1989), pp. 66–7.

Part II
Steve Lacy: in Derek Bailey, *Improvisation: Its Nature and Practice in Music* (British Library National Sound Archive, 1992), p. 54.

Chapter 7
Jerome Harris: in Ingrid Monson, *Saying Something: Jazz Improvisation and Interaction* (Chicago, 1996).

Chapter 8
Duke Ellington: widely quoted.

Chapter 9
Lee Konitz: in Paul Berliner, *Thinking in Jazz: The Infinite Art of Improvisation* (Chicago, 1994), p. 63.

Chapter 10
Barry Green: *The Inner Game of Music* (London, 1986), p. 104.

Chapter 11
Ornette Coleman: quoted in G. Santoro, *Dancing in your Head* (New York, 1994), p. 138.

Chapter 12
Miles Davis: quoted in Ian Carr, *Miles Davis* (London, 1984), p. 73.

Part III
Trevor Tomkins: drummer and jazz educator.

Chapter 13
Wayne Shorter: interviewed in *Jazz Journal*, March 1996.

Chapter 14
Fenton T. Bott, Head of the National Association of Masters of Dancing, in an article entitled 'Unspeakable Jazz Must Go!', from *Ladies' Home Journal*, December 1921.

Chapter 15
Miss Alice Barrow: issued as 'A Warning to Parents', quoted in an article entitled 'Our Jazz-Spotted Middle West', from *Ladies' Home Journal*, February 1927.

Chapter 16
Lilla Bell Pitts, Vice-President of the US Music Educators' National Conference, from the address 'Music and Modern Youth', quoted in the *Music Educators' Journal*, October 1939.

Chapter 17
Howard Taubman: 'Swing and Mozart too', *New York Times*, 29 December 1940.

Further Reading

There are very few books that cover the early ground of jazz piano at a pace suitable for Grades 1–5. This list offers a few of the many directions to go in after you have completed the work in this book.

Tutors

MARK LEVINE, *The Jazz Piano Book* (Sher Music)

BILL DOBBINS, *The Contemporary Jazz Pianist: A Comprehensive Approach to Keyboard Improvisation*, Volumes 1 and 2 (GAMT Music Press, 1978)

PHIL DEGREG, *Jazz Keyboard Voicings and Harmony* (Jamey Aebersold Jazz Inc.)

TIM RICHARDS, *Improvising Blues Piano* (Schott & Co., 1997)

LEWIS RILEY, *Starting to Improvise Jazz Piano* (Boosey & Hawkes, 1988)

Repertoire

Jamey Aebersold, Play-a-long sets. Many available, including albums of key tunes by (amongst others) Thelonious Monk, Horace Silver, Bill Evans, Cedar Walton, Duke Ellington (Jamey Aebersold Jazz Inc.)

The AB Real Book, C treble-clef edition (Associated Board, 2003)

Real Jazz Standards Fake Book (Hal Leonard)

Real Jazz Classics Fake Book (Hal Leonard)

The New Real Book (Sher Music), especially Volumes 1–3

Jazz Masters Series (Wise Publications)

Background information

Ian Carr, Digby Fairweather and Brian Priestley, *Jazz, The Rough Guide: The Essential Companion to Albums and Artists* (Rough Guide Ltd, 1995)

CD Track Listing

Pianists: Charles Beale, Nikki Iles
Drums: Trevor Tomkins
Bass: Tim Wells
Balance Engineer: Ken Blair
Producer: Charles Beale

Digitally recorded and edited DDD

Recorded at Studio 1, Department of Music, University of Surrey, Guildford 18 October 1997

A bmp production for ABRSM (Publishing) Limited

General Index